SATAN
UNMASKED

— THE —
TRUTH
BEHIND THE
— LIE —

29
54
97
108
-167 "It is not about accepting blame; it is about accepting responsibility."

Page

SATAN
UNMASKED

— THE —
TRUTH
BEHIND THE
— LIE —

DR. JAMES B.
RICHARDS

Unless otherwise indicated, all Scripture quotations are from the authorized King James Version.

Scripture quotations marked (NKJV) are from the New King James Version, © 1979, 1980, 1982 by Thomas Nelson, Inc.

Scripture quotations marked (NIV) are from the Holy Bible, New International Version, © 1973, 1978, 1984 by International Bible Society.

Scripture quotations marked (AMP) are from the Amplified New Testament, © 1954, 1958, 1987, by the Lockman Foundation, or are from the Amplified

Bible, Old Testament, © 1962, 1964 by Zondervan Publishing House.

Scripture quotations marked (NLT) are from the New Living Translation, © 1996, Tyndale House Publishers, Inc.

Scripture quotations marked (TLB) are from The Living Bible, © 1971 by Tyndale House Publishers, Wheaton, Illinois.

Word studies, unless otherwise indicated, were done with Thayer's Greek-English Lexicon of the New Testament, written by Carl Ludwig Wilibald

Grimm, trans. and ed. by Joseph Henry Thayer (Grand Rapids, Michigan: Baker Book House, 1977), and Gesenius' Hebrew and Chaldee Lexicon to the Old Testament Scriptures (Grand Rapids, Michigan: Baker Book House, 1979).

SATAN UNMASKED: THE TRUTH BEHIND THE LIE

Revised Edition

ISBN 0-924748-30-3

Printed in the United States of America © 1998, 2004 by Dr. James B. Richards

(Previously published under ISBN 0-924748-12-5 by Impact Ministries.)

Milestones International Publishers is an Imprint of True Potential, Inc.

400 South Main Street, Travelers Rest, SC 29690

http://www.truepotentialmedia.com

1 2 3 4 5 6 7 8 9 10 11 / 09 08 07 06 05 04

DEDICATION

This book is dedicated, with deep appreciation, to my friend and partner Jim Rill. Jim has helped expand my opportunity to take the message of God's love, power, and protection to a whole new group of people. Because of his skill, encouragement, and efforts, this book and the freedom it brings is in your hands today.

CONTENTS

INTRODUCTION

Late one night in the early 1970s, there came a knock at my door. I scrambled out of bed and rushed downstairs to find a nearly hysterical woman and her husband huddled together on my front porch. They kept looking over their shoulders as if they were being followed. Everything about their behavior communicated an infectious fear. Their demeanor brought me in contact with a fear that was palpable. In just seconds I too was caught up in the emotion of the moment!

Her eyes were swollen from crying. He was speaking in half sentences that made no real sense as he continued to look over his shoulder, as if at any moment someone would lunge from the bushes and attack him. I glanced out into the street and saw nothing. Yet, a chill rushed up my spine. I quickly brought them into my living room and closed the door, lest the thing that seemed to be pursuing them attack us all. Their story unfolded into a bizarre experience that would tempt any believer to run and hide. Ironically, it all started earlier in the evening when they attended a seminar about spiritual warfare.

What should have been an evening of ministry about Jesus ended in gross exaggeration of the devil's power. This couple had walked with God for years with a limited knowledge of the finished work of Jesus, and now they feared for their lives. They felt sure that they were no match for Satan's power. They felt that this knowledge somehow brought them to a new level of threat. That night was the beginning of weeks of personal ministry and teaching about the finished work of Jesus. That night also inspired me to search the Scriptures to gain a more realistic view of Satan, our defeated foe. It was the first of hundreds of ministry sessions with good people who lost sight of the truth behind the lie!

In the early 1970s the church seemed to awaken to a new awareness of the devil. It was, unarguably, essential that we come to a better awareness of Satan and his strategies. But it seemed that the truth about the devil was somehow buried behind a lie. Our view of the devil and his power became so exaggerated that it rivaled the truth about the finished work of Jesus. People, like the couple in my living room that night, left seminars about the devil afraid and confused. They no longer trusted Jesus as their Lord and protector. They became devil-conscious and lost their God-consciousness.

I, like many people, went through a period of fear and anxiety as well, not knowing the truth from the lie. I too have been drawn into some of the extremes about the devil. But in the back of my mind I kept asking, "How can this be true if Jesus really did what the Bible said He did?"

After years of preaching the Gospel, traveling around the world, and encountering nearly every form of opposition from witch doctors to Satanists, I have come to the realization that most of what we have believed about the devil is not true. He is the father of all lies. And the greatest lie that he continues to perpetuate is about him and his power.

The grand lie, which is the one thing he is good at, is very cleverly disguised. It contains just enough truth that to challenge the lie seems to challenge the truth! We use scriptures that portray him prior to the resurrection and assume that to be his present standing. These portrayals were true at one time, but today they are lies. We attempt to understand him through the testimonies of those who at one time followed him. The truth and the lie become so entwined that only the Word of God, like a two-edged sword, can sever the two.

The presently accepted beliefs about the devil are, for the most part, religious myths that stand in opposition to the death, burial, and resurrection of Jesus. Instead of giving us faith, they rob us of faith. Instead of giving us confidence, they make us fearful and intimidated. The Gospel will never make us feel fearful, inadequate, or intimidated! *"For God has not given us a spirit of fear* [intimidation], *but of power and of love and of a sound mind"* (2 Timothy 1:7 NKJV).

The following pages may not answer every question about the devil. They will, however, expose many of the myths that have robbed us of confidence, peace, and power. These myths have taken our focus away from Jesus and His finished work and put our attention on the enemy. As you read these pages you will see the truth that is hidden behind the lie of his greatness and power. You will never again fear the devil. You will no longer be subject to his devices. You will see him in his rightful place—under your feet!

CHAPTER 1

TRADITION VS. TRUTH

Tradition is an incredibly powerful tool. In fact, Jesus said it was so powerful that it could make the Word of God have no effect in your life.[1] This neutralizing effect happens when tradition becomes as much a part of our belief system as the Word of God. Tradition is the product of the ideas and perceptions that have been repeated so frequently that they become accepted as reality. Once this happens, they are as important to us as the Bible itself. Tradition is not something about which we are passive. It is something we attempt to guard, maintain, and defend. It is a part of who we are. We understand ourselves through our traditions; therefore, we fight to preserve them.

Tradition becomes a part of our emotional fabric through a simple mental process. Once we accept a certain opinion, the mind begins to seek equilibrium. In other words, if you believe it to be true, the mind seeks to prove it is true. In fact, if you do not determine something to be false and you continually expose yourself to the idea or behavior, it will, in time, be determined to be acceptable and factual. This is the subtlety of deceit.

This isn't something that happens on a mere emotional level. Your mind works till your beliefs and your sense of reality

---

1.   Mark 7:9-13.

are well balanced. There is a set of nerves at the base of the skull called the Reticular Activating System. Once we accept something or pass a judgment, activity in this area of the brain affects our reasoning process. A neurological process begins in our brain to establish it as fact. It alters our ability to perceive. It literally causes us to see it as we believe it to be. I call this process "selective reasoning."

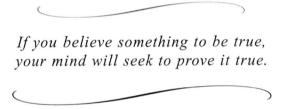

If you believe something to be true, your mind will seek to prove it true.

In selective reasoning we stop seeing things as they are and seek to prove what we have already chosen to believe. It is like looking at a word and thinking it says "horse." You read the sentence over and over again and finally realize that it says "house." You could have sworn that it said h-o-r-s-e. Why were you so sure, yet so wrong? Your mind had already determined what it was seeing.

Does Your Tradition Make God's Word Ineffective?

Jesus identified tradition as a powerful force that must be dealt with if the Word of God is to have power in our lives. He stated that the Pharisees accepted tradition and rejected the Word of God. The *New International Version* says it this way: *"Thus you nullify the word of God by your tradition that you have handed down"* (Mark 7:13). Their tradition "dis-empowered" or neutralized the Word of God in their lives. The Word was still true, but it had no effect. Yet, they were certain they were serving God to the letter of perfection.

When we think of people who have problems with tradition, we tend to think more of the denominational people who are somewhat stuck in their hundred-year-old programs. Or we think of those who are very conservative in their approach to Christian faith. However, many of the more contemporary groups have equally strong traditions. Those traditions might not be as old, but they are just as restrictive as those of the older denominations.

Our traditions begin the moment we insist that we see. The moment a new paradigm is established, we have begun to form a new tradition. It is at that moment that we become blind to anything other than our point of view. Once it is accepted as truth, we begin a process of unquestioned repetition until we can't conceive of any other point of view.

The Pharisees heard the message of God's love and forgiveness, yet they insisted their doctrine was right. Because they clung to their point of view, they could never see what the Scriptures really said. Thus they not only rejected the truth, they also crucified the One who brought the truth. *"Some Pharisees who were with him heard him say this and asked, 'What? Are we blind too?' Jesus said, 'If you were blind, you would not be guilty of sin; but now that you claim you can see, your guilt remains'"* (John 9:40-41 NIV). Insisting that we see is the road to blindness and tradition. Once something is accepted as fact, it is acted upon without thought or questioning.

All that we must do to see is to honestly "consider other possibilities." The Word of God holds so many possibilities to which we have already closed our mind. Therefore it is impossible to see them. We are so consumed with defending our position that we, like the Pharisees, crucify those who bring the truth that will set us free. We must relieve ourselves of the need to prove we are right. Do not place so much of your self-worth on being right. What I see about any subject may be right or wrong. It may have nuggets of truth as well as

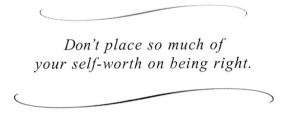

*Don't place so much of
your self-worth on being right.*

nuggets of error. Being right or wrong changes neither who I am in Jesus nor my position before those to whom I minister. We place far too much emphasis on the need to be right and too little emphasis on the need to serve and build up.

Finding the Truth About the Devil

In order to see the devil as he is, we must look at the scriptures that we know are about him. We often attempt to grasp what we do not know, or even have the means to know. We must focus on what is certain and separate fact from assumption. We should not feel a need to create doctrine about what we do not know. If we do not know, we do not know. God will still be our God if we do not have all the answers. If the Bible is not clear on an issue, then God obviously did not feel that it was important enough for elaboration. If God did not elaborate, neither should we.

The law of "first reference" is essential to discovering any truth. We should go back as far in time as possible to discover the truth about the devil. We should look at the earliest references to determine how we must view his beginning. Then we should look to what Jesus accomplished through His death, burial, and resurrection to understand who he is today. Many of the current doctrinal concepts of Satan start with facts. However, they quickly enter into the realm of speculation and ultimately come into conflict with the finished work of Jesus.

In the following chapters we shall deal with the commonly accepted myths concerning the identity of Satan. The most destructive error is not that which is completely false. No! The most diabolical deception is the one that contains just enough truth to make the lie pass under the radar screen undetected or, in this case, unquestioned. Within each myth there is a degree of absolute truth. The challenging aspect of sorting this out will be the refusal to attempt to support the myth with the truth.

In order to get to the truth, we will begin with how Satan came into being. In these passages of Scripture we will seek to unravel the lie that is hidden behind the truth. In so doing we will gain a more scriptural concept of who Satan really is. Understanding his origins can give us clear insights into how he thinks and functions, and ultimately how he attempts to work in our lives.

Isaiah 14 and Ezekiel 28 are accepted by the majority of scholars as the definitive source for understanding Satan's fall. We will look at these passages and identify what we should clearly accept. Likewise, we will attempt to identify the speculation and subsequent tradition that we have accepted along with the facts. In so doing we will discover the tradition that has caused us to create a larger-than-life concept of the devil. I want us to look at Satan's fall and understand who he was in eternity and where his fall places him today.

Make it your prayer to have eyes that see and ears that hear. Make a determination that you will only see the devil as he is through the finished work of Jesus.

CHAPTER 2

THE WORSHIP LEADER MYTH

O ne of the most commonly accepted theories about the
devil is the worship leader theory. Like other false assumptions, it robs God of His glory and robs man of his digni-
ty. This theory says that Satan, prior to his fall, was the
worship leader in heaven. Many people go to extravagant
lengths in their attempt to describe who he was and what his
function was. This theory takes the verse that says, "*Thou art
the anointed cherub that covereth*" (Ezekiel 28:14), and takes a
quantum leap to say, "Satan covered the throne of God."

This commonly accepted assumption is not supported in
any scripture. But like all assumptions, once accepted as true,
they alter the way we see other things. Ezekiel 28:13 says, "*the
workmanship of thy tabrets and of thy pipes was prepared in thee.*"
This is where this assumption is developed. Since pipes and
tabrets are musical instruments, it is assumed that he was a
living musical instrument that existed to provide praise and
worship for God. From here, those who embrace this theory
extrapolate beyond reality.

I like to remind people that this passage is about his
splendor. It goes to great lengths to describe the precious
stones that were his covering. The words *tabrets* and *pipes* are
both words that can be used to describe settings into which
precious stones are placed. The word *tabret* is more commonly
translated as "timbrel," but in this context it would use the

second translation as a setting for a precious stone. Thus, the idea of a living musical instrument begins to lose its logic when taken in context.

The context of scripture does not support Satan's being a worship leader.

This theory is further developed by the phrase, *"the anointed cherub that covereth."* Starting from the assumption that he was a worship leader becomes the perspective from which other scriptures are interpreted. If he was the worship leader, he must have covered the throne of God. These two assumptions seem to answer the questions about these passages. In light of the previously accepted theory, it makes sense.

This theory, however, presents an image of Satan that makes him closer to God than anyone in heaven. Again, this is completely inconsistent with what we do know about God in eternity. John 1:1 says, *"In the beginning was the Word, and the Word was with God."* "The Word" refers to Jesus. It says He was with God, or literally "face to face" with God. There was no one closer to God the Father than Jesus. Satan was not the one closest to God. Satan was not the one closest to the throne of God. To place Satan in this intimate relationship with God dethrones the Lord Jesus.

It is a myth that Satan was the worship leader in heaven, the leader in praise to God. It simply is not borne out by the Scriptures. So what else do we "believe" about the devil that is a myth?

CHAPTER 3

THE SATANIC MUSIC MYTH

M usic is an issue that has been debated from the earliest
history of the church. Much of the dogma surrounding
music emerges from the tradition of Satan's being a worship
leader. Developing a doctrine that starts with the worship
leader myth makes it all sound logical. However, when we remove the assumption that Satan was a worship leader, the
ideas lose all scriptural logic.

The explanation for the power of music is often derived
from this tradition about Satan. If he was the leader of worship, then he obviously uses music powerfully. Some have
gone as far as designating certain "beats" to the devil. Some
have said that if the harmony is more prevalent than the
melody, it is of the devil. Others have said that if the tempo is
too predominant, it is of the devil. Some have rejected music
altogether. Some have said we must play the music backwards
to see if it is of the devil. None of this is scripturally valid.

The devil did not create music. In fact, he did not create
anything. He has no creative powers. God created all things,
and He created all things for good. Men may pervert what
God has created, but nothing is evil in and of itself. Only a
wicked heart can make something wicked. Titus 1:15 says,
"Unto the pure all things are pure: but unto them that are defiled

and unbelieving is nothing pure; but even their mind and conscience is defiled."

As I listen to people describe the difference between anointed music and demonic music, it always seems to be a matter of taste and preference. Whatever I prefer must be the anointed music. It seems that Christians have little tolerance for individual taste. Additionally, we have the need to justify all our personal preferences by giving them spiritual significance. We feel it is justifiable to enjoy something only if we can prove that it is of God. The truth is that some people prefer one style while others prefer something else. The lyrics, not the style, determine whether it is good or evil.

*The lyrics, not the style,
determine whether music is good or evil.*

According to many of today's theological definitions, some of the psalms would have been New Age, compromising, and demonic. The Psalms contain the first "contemporary gospel" music. The psalmist took a psalm inspired of God and set it to a tune that was already popular in his day. The introductory notes to Psalm 84 in *The Amplified Bible* say, "To the Chief Musician; set to a Philistine lute, or [possibly] a particular Gittite tune. A Psalm of the sons of Korah."

In this instance the psalmist wrote a song inspired of God and accompanied it with a tune that the Philistines were singing in the bars. To say it another way, he took a popular, worldly tune that someone else wrote and inserted the words of God, making it quickly accepted by the people. Many of our old, much-loved hymns were inspired words placed to bar room music of that day. Yet, today they are considered sacred. It is only because of continual exposure that they became a part of our culture, our tradition.

Many of the psalms were as contemporary as it gets. Therefore, my personal taste does not determine if a song is either demonically inspired or anointed. It is all right to like or dislike any style. We do not have to validate our preferences or justify our dislikes from a doctrinal perspective. As Paul told the Gentile believers, if something violates your conscience, don't do it. However, don't make it a standard of righteousness for others or turn it into a doctrine.[1] If the Scriptures are unclear, follow your own conscience.

If we are so out of touch that we have to play a song backwards to understand it or analyze the beat to determine its source, we have already lost the battle. It is very simple to identify the source of a song. Just listen to the words. What is the message?

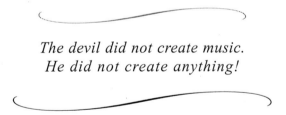

The devil did not create music.
He did not create anything!

Some have said, "Yes, the words are good, but that beat makes me think of sensual things." Then, may I suggest that you have a personal problem? It is typical codependent, legalistic thinking that always desires to place the responsibility for our problems on someone else. The devil did not create music. He did not create anything. When anything gets perverted, it

---

1.   See Romans 14 and 1 Corinthians 8.

gets perverted in the hearts of men. We, rather than deal with a wicked heart, try to make the music perverted.

Worship leaders and musicians have been beaten to death with the theory of the "luciferian spirit." I have heard preachers say, "You have to watch those musicians. The luciferian spirit will come on them. After all, Lucifer was the worship leader in heaven." The ego problems of musicians can be addressed much more effectively by dealing with the real problem. There is little value in creating super-spiritual concepts that only serve to condemn and destroy. If the worship isn't working, it is not working. If the worship leader has an ego problem associated with his music, then deal with it for what it is: an attitude problem.

There are no special demons for music. Instead, music is simply a powerful tool that God created to have a profound effect on the souls of men. It can affect them for good or evil. David played music to Saul to soothe his soul. When he did, the evil spirit left the king.[2] Music has always been an important factor for praise and worship in every generation. History reveals that those unique individuals who make worship more contemporary are much more effective at reaching their generation.

It is a myth that music is demonically controlled. It is not heresy to enjoy the type of music that your taste runs to.

---

2.   See 1 Samuel 16:23.

CHAPTER 4

THE MYTH OF DUALISM

One of the most common, dis-empowering misconceptions of the devil presents him in a life-and-death struggle with God over the world. We somehow get the idea that the outcome has not yet been determined and that the souls of all men hang in the balance. Nothing could be further from the truth. The souls of men hang in the balance of their own decisions, but the outcome of the battle between God and the devil was determined when Jesus rose from the dead and stripped him of all power and might.

We know that Satan was not originally who he is today. He was not always the accuser of the brethren. He was not always the one attempting to overthrow God. There was a time when Satan was a cherub. The Bible says he was *"the anointed cherub that covereth"* (Ezekiel 28:14).

There are many theories about Satan's fall, about who he is and what he did before his fall. Most of the accepted theories concerning Satan's identity unwittingly deny the Word of God and the cross of Christ. A common flaw in the doctrine of Satan unwittingly minimizes God as the Creator and exalts Satan as a rival creator. This false premise creates a dualistic concept of two, near equal rivals fighting for the destiny of man. It is essential that we understand that Satan and God are *not* equal in power. Neither are they near equal in power.

There is no comparison between the two beings. Satan is a created being. God is the Creator. Satan was, in fact, an angel. He was an angel who is now fallen from the lofty position he once held. He is a failure. He is a "has been." Any glory and dominion he may have once had is now lost.

Satan is not and never was equal in power with God.

Satan is a defeated foe. His only avenue into the world is through the hearts of deceived or otherwise corrupt people who give him place in their lives.

In our tradition, Satan is presented as a powerful, orderly, wise opponent against whom we stand powerless, unless we use the name of Jesus with enough faith, authority, and vocal prominence. Satan is not wise, however. After knowing God in eternity, he attempted to overthrow His kingdom. (Not a real show of wisdom.) Despite having thousands of years to see the Scriptures and see God's Word continually prevail, he still motivated the crucifixion of Jesus, which brought about his ultimate defeat. History records his folly. He never wins. He knows he cannot win.

As we examine Satan's character, we will see that he is blinded by pride, fear, jealousy, and strife. There is chaos in his ranks. His kingdom is in disarray. He cannot maintain order. Those of his kingdom murder one another. He is in a panic, for he knows that he has only a short time.[1]

---

1.   See Revelation 12:12.

Following these dualistic concepts, some have presented Satan as the lord of hell. They see hell as some place over which he is the ruler supreme. This theory has been taken so far as to present Satan as the one who tormented Jesus in hell after the crucifixion. Satan isn't lord of anything. He has never been to hell (the lake of fire and brimstone). When he goes to hell, he will never come out. He will not be the tormentor in hell. He will be the one who *experiences* the ultimate of torment! And not the least of it will be his own personal delusion of foolishness in thinking that a created being could ever overthrow the Creator.

When taken to its ultimate conclusion, the concept of dualism presents a tug of war between God and the devil that leaves man a helpless victim trapped between two superpowers. It over-exalts the devil, minimizes God, denies the finished work of Jesus, and corrupts the position of man.

CHAPTER 5

THE MYTH OF SATAN'S PREEMINENCE OVER MAN

M an plays a key role of importance to God. Some ideologies see man as non-essential or of no importance to God. What they fail to grasp is God's extreme value and love for man. He considers man to be precious. We are the object of His great affection. Many doctrines about the devil cleverly minimize God's view of man.

Beginning with the worship leader theory, we take a quantum leap into many unstable, unscriptural concepts regarding the devil. Let us take a moment to recap the progression. Ezekiel 28:14 says, *"Thou art the anointed cherub that covereth; and I have set thee so: thou wast upon the holy mountain of God; thou hast walked up and down in the midst of the stones of fire."* We know Satan covered something. The problem is that we do not know what he covered. Unfounded assumptions lead us to believe that he covered the throne of God. This verse does not say or otherwise indicate what he covered; it simply states that he covered something.

If we assume that he covered the throne of God, several wrong assumptions immediately emerge. The first wrong assumption is that he was a worship leader. The second wrong assumption is that he covered the throne of God. The third is that he was more intimate with God than any other being. To follow this logic leads to many possibilities that I feel are completely inconsistent with what we know about God. We must realize that any area of our doctrinal belief will affect other areas of belief. What I believe about Satan will ultimately influence what I believe about God. If my beliefs about the devil force me to have inconsistent beliefs about God, then I must reevaluate those beliefs.

To continue with that train of thought brings us to the wild assumption that because Satan was the worship leader who fell, a subsequent need was created in heaven. Out of this need God created man to replace a fallen worship leader. Once again this violates what we know to be true about God. God is love. All of His actions are motivated by and governed by love.

*If your beliefs regarding God
are inconsistent, then you should
reevaluate your beliefs about Satan.*

The Amplified Bible translates God's love as self-sacrificial. This *agape* love always looks to meet the needs of others. It is never motivated by selfish ambition or need. Selfishness and self-centeredness is the heart of sin. If God created man out of need, He acted inconsistent with His nature and He committed sin. The New Testament presents love as the motivating factor in God's creation of man, not need. Because of these presumptive theories, some people actually see God as a self-centered tyrant who heartlessly uses mankind as mere pawns to gratify His selfish needs.

men replaced ?

The idea that Satan replaced man leads to questions about his authority on planet Earth. God gave dominion of planet Earth to man. If we are simply replacements, then it would lead to the possibility that Earth belongs to Satan and that he is attempting to reclaim what was rightfully his before the fall.

The reality is that Satan has no authority over you.

Possibly the most destructive of all the Satan myths is the theory that Satan has some degree of authority on earth. Authority is about rights. This theory presents a dis-empowering concept that says when we sin, we give Satan the right, or the authority, to attack us. Probably no other doctrine has plunged man into legalism and away from faith in God than this.

When Jesus came out of the grave, He said, "*All authority in heaven and on earth has been given to me*" (Matthew 28:18 NIV). The definitive statement leaves no room for question. He did not say some authority. He did not say all authority unless we sin. Our actions cannot violate the victory that Jesus won by His death, burial, and resurrection. He has *all* authority (right). Satan has no authority, and there is nothing we can do to "give him the right" to attack us.

Powerful!

We can, however, refuse to believe what we have in Jesus. We can accept Satan's attack as legitimate. The reality is, nevertheless, that Satan has no authority over me or you or any lost person. Ignorance, unbelief, and tradition become the means whereby we yield to his torment. All of that can stop today as you read these words.

I am sure that by now one of your doctrines has been challenged. Perhaps you are angry. You may be ready to "prove your position," and if that is what you intend to do, then that is what you will do. But I tell you, there is something here for you to see. Unfortunately, you cannot see it if you insist that you already see.

By the end of this book you will have the opportunity to be free from the fear of the devil to a degree that you may have never known. You will have the opportunity to experience joy and peace in the Lord in new dimensions. You will find a doctrinal consistency that will end the confusion about the devil. My only advice to you is, *just consider*!

CHAPTER 6

SATAN IS A BLIND FOOL

To understand anything, we must start from what we know to be fact. There are many clearly established facts that we have about Satan and his fall. These facts must be the starting place. If we begin from an assumption, we mistakenly use the Scriptures to prove that assumption.

In our School of Ministry, I give the students some essential rules for interpretation. First, never start from the obscure. Start from the obvious, then see if the obscure supports it. Equally important is that it is better to know nothing than to assume something to be true. If we assume, we place ourselves in a position to constantly prove and protect our assumption. This usually leads to ever-growing confusion and error.

Openness is an essential quality for a student of the Word of God. To admit that we are unsure or do not know creates an openness that can see other possibilities. To accept a certain belief, yet stay open to other possibilities, makes one teachable. We know the Word of God is absolute, but we know our understanding of the Word is not.

Let's look at the Scriptures to discover some absolutes about the devil. Let's see if we can find a starting place for understanding who he is, how he functions, and why he fell. Let us open our eyes so that we can see him as he is instead of how we assume him to be. We should not be *"ignorant of his devices"* (2 Corinthians 2:11).

Pride Was Satan's Downfall

First Timothy 3 talks about the essential character traits for a person who functions in the office of a bishop. These qualities need to be operative in his life to protect him and his followers. Verse 6 says that a person desiring to be a bishop should not be *"a novice, lest being lifted up with pride he fall into the condemnation of the devil."* The word *condemnation* can have many possible meanings. One translation can simply be "decision." Although there could be other possibilities, let's consider the word *condemnation*, in this context, to be decision.

This is saying, then, that a person wanting to be in the ministry should not be a novice, lest he get lifted up with pride and fall into the decision of the devil. Even if you leave that to mean condemnation, it is okay. The main issue is the role pride played in causing the devil to fall into condemnation. His pride determined the way he made rationalized decisions. His decisions brought about his fall. His present state of condemnation is the result of his pride.

*Pride put Satan into his
present state of condemnation.*

This passage goes on to say, *"Moreover he must have a good report of them which are without; lest he fall into reproach and the snare of the devil"* (verse 7). Pride was the factor that caused Satan to fall. It was the motivating force behind his decision-making.

This is fact, not assumption. Pride corrupted his judgment and thereby caused Satan to fall into a trap. Although pride has many destructive characteristics and consequences, blindness may be the ultimate.

Pride produces a warped paradigm that places "me" at the center of my reasoning process. With me at the center I become very confused about the true issues and the consequences. My reasoning is "me centered" and not God centered. It distorts my ability to see and thereby make sound decisions.

Rather than Satan's being the all-wise ruler we had assumed him to be, he is in fact a maniac deceived and blinded by his pride. He doesn't see anything as it is. He sees things through eyes that are blinded by pride. He is so blinded that after having known God as only the angels know God, he thought that he should be God. He thought that he could become God. So Satan's problem was pride.

A Closer Look at Pride

Let's look at Psalm 31 as we consider pride and its ramifications. Verse 20 says, *"Thou shalt hide them in the secret of thy presence from the pride of man: thou shalt keep them secretly in a pavilion from the strife of tongues."* We know pride will always create strife. Anytime you are in strife with someone, one or both of you is operating in pride. Usually all it takes for strife to leave a situation is for one person to choose to stop walking in pride and start walking in love.

Psalm 36:11 says, *"Let not the foot of pride come against me, and let not the hand of the wicked remove me."* Pride is a destructive force. It is not passive. When you have pride in your life, you will find yourself coming against or attacking other people.

You will attack the people who threaten your false sense of self. Pride is fueled by insecurity. It is the mask worn by those who have a faltering self-worth.

One earmark of a person who is insecure is that he will function in pride. We have always thought of insecurity as the fear to make a decision. That is, no doubt, one manifestation of insecurity. Another manifestation of insecurity is a person always having to be right, or having to look perfect. This person is easily threatened when questioned or challenged. Pride comes against others when threatened. It always lashes out. You always find insecure people attacking, fighting, arguing, and attempting to maintain the appearance of being right. They are caught in a snare.

Psalm 73:6 says, *"Therefore pride compasseth them about as a chain; violence covereth them as a garment."* We know that pride becomes violent. One characteristic we know about the devil is that violence was found in him. Pride, if followed to its end, will bring one to violence. Force, therefore, stands in opposition to the person who is a true leader. Force is a diabolical fruit of pride.

Proverbs 8:13 says, *"The fear of the LORD is to hate evil: pride, and arrogancy, and the evil way, and the froward mouth, do I hate."* The word for "fear" in the Hebrew is a word that is translated to reverently love and worship God. Thus this verse could read, "The reverent love and worship of the Lord is to hate evil, pride...." The reason the lover of God hates pride is because pride is a trait of the devil. It opposes God and puts self at the center of the equation.

In pride we are going to see arrogance and a froward or crooked mouth, a crooked tongue—a tongue that does not speak truth properly. It does not yield to God. Pride exalts self above God. It makes me the god of my world.

Proverbs 11:2 says, *"When pride cometh, then cometh shame: but with the lowly is wisdom."* A person of pride will always have shame. Pride is so blinding that it cannot find the truth. Pride cannot see the way to true victory. The heart of pride is so caught up with maintaining the illusions of victory and power that it cannot find the reality. This inability to see the truth through the eyes of pride is what leads to failure and shame. Satan is the ultimate model of pride, failure, and shame.

> *Satan is the ultimate model*
> *of pride, failure, and shame.*
> *He is the epitome of a blind fool.*

Proverbs 13:10 says, *"Only by pride cometh contention: but with the well advised is wisdom."* This is an interesting contrast of thought. People with pride have contention. The well-advised have wisdom. The person of pride can never be advised because he is interested in how it looks. He pretends to have it all figured out. Jesus told the Pharisees that they were blind because they insisted that they could see. Pride prevents us from receiving the wisdom of God. When we insist that we see we make it impossible to hear the voice of God or man. If one is to receive instruction, he must first admit the need for instruction. Pride prohibits admitting need. Satan is not an "all-wise being"; rather, he is the epitome of a blind fool.

Let's not follow in those footsteps.

CHAPTER 7

MAN IS A SUPERIOR BEING

How we see ourselves in relation to God affects how we see ourselves in relation to all other beings. It is only as we properly grasp our relationship to God that our relationships with the rest of creation come into proper alignment. Thus the fact that we—unlike all other beings—were created in the likeness and image of God firmly establishes our preeminence to all other created beings. We are the children of God. We are the heirs of God. It was for us, not the angels, that Jesus died. It was God's special love for us that placed us at the center of the eternal vortex of God's attention. If we had no other facts, this alone would be sufficient to show us that we are not now, nor ever have been, inferior to the devil. But the Bible is rich with supporting evidence that refutes any conjecture to the contrary.

Satan Is Inferior to Man

In trying to understand our present relationship to Satan, let us look at what our relationship to him would have been if he had not fallen. Hebrews 2:6 says, *"But one in a certain place testified, saying, What is man, that thou art mindful of him? or the son of man, that thou visitest him?"* In other words, "God, what is man to You?" Verse 7 continues, *"Thou madest him a little lower than the angels."* In the original language of Psalm 8 (which this passage in Hebrews quotes), the word *angels* is translated from the Hebrew word *Elohim*, which is used to describe the Trinity.

Looking at Psalm 8:5, then, this passage of the Scriptures is saying that man was created just a little lower than the Godhead. This means that Satan has always been an inferior being to mankind. Even if Satan had been the worship leader (which he was not), and even if he did cover the throne of God (which he did not), the Bible still says that man was created just a little lower than Elohim. We were created in the likeness and image of God. We know God in a way that Satan has never known Him. Our splendor is far greater than that of any of the angels.

At this juncture many are quick to point out that man fell from his position. However, so did Satan! Nevertheless, let's continue. Hebrews 1:14 says of the angels, *"Are they not all ministering spirits, sent forth to minister for them who shall be heirs of salvation?"* Lucifer was an angel, possibly an archangel. As an archangel, he would have been head over all the servant angels for mankind. He would not rule over man; he would serve man. Even at the height of glory, even if he had never fallen, all he would ever be is a servant.

We are sons of God, and
Satan is an out-of-work servant.

Both Satan and man fell, yes. Man, though, has been redeemed. We have been made righteous. Our present position with God is not beneath what Adam had; it is far superior to Adam. We are the children of God. We are flesh of His flesh. We are royalty. Satan, on the other hand, is and forevermore will be a fallen angel who was created to serve us. This means that we are sons of God and he is an out-of-work servant.

Satan Has No Authority

Likewise, we know that Jesus was raised up triumphant over death and hell. We know that He took the keys of death and hell. We know that He now has all authority. This means that Satan has no authority, no rights whatsoever.[1]

Satan is not above us.
He is under our feet.

Ephesians 1:21-23 explains the position of Jesus as *"far above all principality, and power, and might, and dominion, and every name that is named, not only in this world, but also in that which is to come: and hath put all things under his feet, and gave him to be the head over all things to the church, which is his body, the fulness of him that filleth all in all."* The Bible teaches that we are "in Christ." So where does that put us? We are in a joint position with Jesus far above all other principalities, power, and might.

Colossians 3:1-3 gives this direction: *"Since, then, you have been raised with Christ, set your hearts on things above, where Christ is seated at the right hand of God. Set your minds on things above, not on earthly things. For you died, and your life is now hidden with Christ in God"* (NIV). Since we are raised up with Christ, our old sinful man is dead. Since we are hid in Him, that is where we focus our hearts, minds, and thoughts. We must see ourselves from this heavenly perspective. Because we are in Christ, we are above Satan. Satan is under our feet. He is not above us. He has no authority over us.

---

1. See Matthew 28 and Hebrews 2.

There are many other present tense realities about Satan, but for our purposes we shall end with the following. Although Satan is presented as a super-strategic being with many levels of principality and power, the Scriptures actually portray something quite different. I am fully aware of the passage in Ephesians that speaks of principality and power, but we must understand this scripture in light of what Colossians says about the resurrection of Jesus. *"And having spoiled principalities and powers, he made a show of them openly, triumphing over them in it"* (Colossians 2:15).

Jesus *"spoiled"* principality and power. He triumphed over, conquered, disarmed, and dismantled whatever structure there was to Satan's kingdom. In forthcoming chapters we will review this more closely. It is sufficient to say at this point, however, that our concept of the strategic, organized kingdom of Satan cannot be as we had thought.

When Jesus' time to depart planet Earth grew close, He taught the disciples many essential realities. In so doing He gave them the tools they would need to thrive in a hostile world. Among the many incredible things Jesus taught, one of the most profound is in John 17:22 when He said, *"The glory which thou gavest me I have given them"*! Jesus left no doubt concerning man's preeminence in planet Earth.

CHAPTER 8

THE FALL OF SATAN

U nderstanding Satan's fall provides us with insight into his weakness of character and, to some degree, his continued strategies. Moreover, it gives us protection against falling into the same trap! It is a spiritual principle that every seed bears after its own kind. Satan is no different; he destroys others with the same venom that destroyed him. By identifying the process whereby he fell from his lofty position, we can come to more quickly identify when we are following that same process.

Let us go to the accepted passages of Scripture describing Satan's fall and gain insight into this bizarre twist of events. As we previously determined, pride led Satan into a decision-making process that led to his fall. Pride is full of envy and jealousy. Satan had several opportunities at jealousy and envy. He could have envied God in all of His glory. Satan could have somehow envisioned himself superior to God. He could have envied the Lord Jesus. After all, He was to be the center of all eternal purpose. Last of all, he could have envied man, the one who would inherit planet Earth and sonship.

Consider the scenario: Man was placed on planet Earth to rule and reign. He was given total and complete authority. Satan had none. Worst of all, Satan was to be a servant to this newly created being who held some special position in the heart of God. When man came on the scene, a being was created and brought to planet Earth who was superior to Satan even at the pinnacle of his glory.

Satan Was on Earth to Serve Man

Let us look a little closer at Satan's relationship to man. Ezekiel 28:14 says, *"Thou art the anointed cherub that covereth."* Virtually all scholars agree that this portion of the Scriptures is speaking of the fall of Satan. From previous study we have established that there is no evidence that he covered the throne of God, as many had assumed. *The New Living Translation* says, beginning in verse 12, *"Son of man, weep for the king of Tyre. Give him this message from the Sovereign LORD: You were the perfection of wisdom and beauty. You were in Eden the garden of God."* This says that Satan was in the Garden of Eden. Eden was in earth, not heaven. *"Your clothing was adorned with every precious stone....They were given to you on the day you were created. I ordained and anointed you as the mighty angelic guardian. You had access to the holy mountain of God..."* (Ezekiel 28:12-14 NLT). Satan was in Eden and had access to heaven.

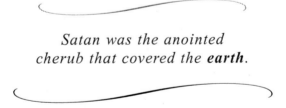

Satan was the anointed
*cherub that covered the **earth**.*

Heaven was not his domain. Earth was his domain, but he had access to heaven. My deduction is that he was not the anointed cherub that covered the throne of God, but the anointed cherub that covered the earth. His realm of covering, dominion, and guardianship was planet Earth, not heaven. He was placed on earth to be the guardian, but instead he became the thief. Rather than serving the heirs, he attempted to destroy the heirs.

Hebrews 1:7 says, *"And of the angels he saith, Who maketh his angels spirits, and his ministers a flame of fire."* Satan was an angel. Angels are spiritual beings that live as ministers or servants. Satan, if he had not fallen, would have spent all of eternity as a servant to mankind. He would have never risen above the position of servant. This presents a much more logical concept of Satan's envy and jealousy. He was inferior to God, the Lord Jesus, and all of mankind.

When Satan came to Adam and Eve in the Garden of Eden, why did he not just kill them? What did he really want? What was he after? The Bible identifies him as the god of this world. Thus it seems he was after the dominion of man and planet Earth.

Satan Wanted Man's Dominion

Satan reasoned himself into deception, rebellion, and destruction. He looked at his beauty, brilliance, and splendor and used this as the basis for his reasoning and rationalizing. Ezekiel 28:17 says, *"Thine heart was lifted up because of thy beauty, thou hast corrupted thy wisdom by reason of thy brightness."* Satan was a glorious creation, but he began to look at all he had going for him and from that point of strength he reasoned. This small morsel contains an incredible seed of wisdom! We should never look at what is right about us to justify wrong actions.

Satan started to reason, and through his reasoning he corrupted his wisdom. The original language is clear about this. The process of reasoning he went through began from an actual fact. Like most deceit, it was built from a basis of fact. Satan looked at the facts about himself and said, "Based on this about me, I can justify these actions. I should be the one to get the honor. I should be the one to have supremacy. I should inherit the earth."

We should never look at what is right about us to justify wrong actions.

The moment you justify your actions from some basis of greatness, you are corrupting your wisdom. Corrupting wisdom always begins from a basis of what is right. You will look at truth about you and say, "Because of this, I am justified in pursuing that. Because I have done all of this right, I am justified in doing you wrong in this area." In other words, you begin to build until you ultimately build beyond truth. When you reason beyond truth, you have corrupted truth.

Satan, the anointed cherub that covered, was in Eden (the Garden of God) and was a wonderful creation that became moved by pride. He looked at himself and became envious and jealous. When Satan came to the Garden of Eden, he did not come to kill man. He wanted to rule over man. He wanted to be a god over man and over planet Earth. He was completely moved with envy and jealousy.

Although there is much we do not know, we now know that his dominion was earth, not heaven. We know that his pride allowed him to justify something that was completely irrational. We know that, at best, he would have served mankind. Nevertheless, no matter what he may have been, we are the heirs of God. We are the glory of God in Jesus. We will rule and reign with Him. Satan is a deceived being who has fallen from any position of grandeur he ever knew.

CHAPTER 9

ACCESS DENIED

T he only tools Satan has to work with are lies and deceit. He has nothing else. Satan does not have the right (authority) to work in anyone's life. It is not authority that creates the opportunity for him; it is ignorance and unbelief. The only opportunity he has is the one I give him.

Satan Came to Heaven to Accuse Men

Satan is found in the book of Job coming before the presence of God. Job 1:6-7 says, *"Now there was a day when the sons of God came to present themselves before the LORD, and Satan came also among them. And the LORD said unto Satan, Whence comest thou? Then Satan answered the LORD, and said, From going to and fro in the earth, and from walking up and down in it."* Satan was not among the angels. He came among them. He came from his habitat, planet Earth.

He came into the presence of God for the specific purpose of accusing Job. The name Satan means "accuser." In the Old Testament, we have a clear picture of Satan appearing before God to accuse the brethren. Like many Old Testament truths, however, we have somehow failed to recognize how they have changed since the resurrection of Jesus. Failure to recognize what has changed from the Old to the New keeps us from being steadfast in the covenant, thereby limiting God in our lives. Jesus brought about many changes. Satan's access to heaven may be one of the most surprising. We brought this Old Testament reality of Satan as the accuser into the New Testament and presented a picture of Jesus and Satan arguing before the throne of God for the souls of men.

There is no question about the souls of men in the New Covenant. Jesus obtained righteousness and gave it to us as a free gift. Our old man has died. We are new creations in Christ Jesus. Therefore Satan has no basis of accusation against us. We are raised up, righteous, made holy, hid in Christ, and free from judgment.

Satan's original fall (where he went from Lucifer to Satan) was not the last of his falls. Even after that fall he had access to the throne of God. Using the law he could accuse men to God on the basis of their actions. We may be surprised, however, to see how his present position has so dramatically changed.

*Satan's status changed
with the advent of the New Covenant.*

Two thousands years ago Jesus made a profound statement. In John 12:31 Jesus said, *"Now is the judgment of this world: now shall the prince of this world be cast out."* Jesus said at that moment the prince of this world would be cast out. Was Satan to be cast out of the world at that moment? No! We know he is still in the world. Rather, through the resurrection Satan would forever be cast out of heaven.

And there was war in heaven: Michael and his angels fought against the dragon; and the dragon fought and his angels, and prevailed not; neither was their place found any more in heaven. And the great dragon was cast out, that old serpent, called the Devil, and Satan, which deceiveth the whole world: he was cast out into the earth, and his angels were cast out with him. And I heard a loud voice saying in heaven, Now is come salvation, and strength, and the kingdom of our God, and the power of his Christ: for the accuser of our brethren is cast down, which accused them before our God day and night (Revelation 12:7-10).

At the same time that salvation came, the accuser of the brethren that accused them before God day and night was *cast down!* Jesus said, before His death, that Satan would be cast out. The book of Revelation describes that event. Salvation came when Jesus was raised from the dead, went into the heavenly holy of holies, purged it with His own blood, and sat down at the right hand of God, signifying that it was complete.

Access Denied!

From the moment Jesus was raised from the dead, Satan was cast out of heaven. He can no longer enter the presence of God to condemn and accuse us. He is denied access! Instead our Intercessor, our Advocate, the One who is for us, is in the presence of God proclaiming our righteousness in Him. In reality, God has never heard one bad thing about you since the day you came to Jesus. He has known you only through Jesus, the One who makes you righteous.

Revelation 12:12 says, "*Therefore rejoice, ye heavens, and ye that dwell in them. Woe to the inhabiters of the earth and of the sea! for the devil is come down unto you, having great wrath, because he knoweth that he hath but a short time.*" While heaven is rejoicing, we inhabitants of the earth must follow our only course of victory. We must have confidence in the finished work of the Lord Jesus Christ. *"And they overcame him by the blood of the Lamb, and by the word of their testimony; and they loved not their lives unto the death"* (Revelation 12:11).

God has not heard one bad thing about you since you were born again.

In a way, this will not be Satan's last fall, for his last fall shall be into the lake of fire and brimstone. His eternal doom is sealed. The end has been declared from the beginning. He is defeated and we are victorious. Christ is no longer in a battle with him. That battle has been won. And as we shall soon see, our battle is not with him, but with our beliefs.

It is time to give up all fear of the enemy. Let us give up our vain attempts to cast him down. Instead, let us accept his consummate defeat at the hands of our Lord and Savior. Let us rejoice in Him and be glad. He has given us a perfect salvation. Let us rejoice in the finished work of Jesus that conquered him who had the power of death, who accused the brethren before God. Let's rejoice that He stripped him of all position and power!

CHAPTER 10

ALL AUTHORITY

It is amazing to see how we could begin with a few wrong assumptions and develop an entire theology around something that is not true. Yet, it has happened. This is, after all, the way Satan operates. He is the master at maintaining just enough truth to hide the lie behind the truth. The lie goes unchallenged because to do so would seem to challenge the truth. It is true that Satan is a factor in this world. However, he is not the factor that our imagination has created. Because we have not known or recognized our enemy or his strategies, we have worked an unsuccessful strategy against him—a strategy that ultimately undermines our faith in the risen Lord. The belief of the lie has seemingly stripped us of the victory that Jesus won through His death, burial, and resurrection. But for you, today, the lie is exposed!

Misunderstandings about the devil are not new. The early church had many misconceptions. Most of these misconceptions were developed from Old Covenant concepts. From the resurrection until now, the church has struggled with the tendency to incorporate the Old Testament into the New. Unfortunately, to do so totally neutralizes the power of the New Covenant in our lives.

The New Covenant Is Just That—New

Under the Old Covenant, if a person fell short in any way, he would rightfully look for the curse of the law on his life. He had a covenant with God that was based on his performance. The promises of that covenant were contingent upon a person's ability to obey. The promises were for those who obeyed; the curses were for those who did not.

The New Covenant, however, is quite different. It is by far a better covenant. Hebrews 8:6 says, *"But now hath he obtained a more excellent ministry, by how much also he is the mediator of a better covenant, which was established upon better promises."* We have a better covenant with better promises. Yet, unbelief and misunderstanding about the New Covenant make us continually look back to the Old Covenant.

We succumb to Satan's method of reasoning and rationalizing, all of which is the product of the carnal mind. Unwittingly, we fall from the place where the covenant is working in our life. After all, it is hard to believe it is actually as good as it promises! It is hard to believe that God is that good. Yet, He is. The question is, do we believe it? Will we develop a theology based on the New Covenant that exceeds all we could think and imagine? Or will we use the Old Covenant to create a theology that fits into our carnal reasoning?

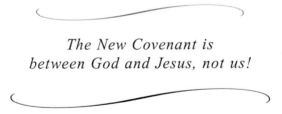

*The New Covenant is
between God and Jesus, not us!*

This New Covenant was not made between God and each individual believer. The New Covenant was between God and Jesus! Galatians 3:16 says, *"Now to Abraham and his seed were the promises made. He saith not, And to seeds, as of many; but as of one, And to thy seed, which is Christ."*

The Old Covenant was based on each individual's ability to uphold his side of the arrangement. The New Covenant, however, is based on *one* man's ability to uphold the agreement. That man was Jesus. He fulfilled all the righteous requirements of the law. He made the covenant sure. It has been sealed by His death. He has risen to ensure that it is enforced to the ultimate extent of every promise. It cannot be changed.

God does not, therefore, uphold His covenant with us on the basis of our ability to always perform properly. Rather, it is based on Jesus. This is why Paul exhorted us to bring every thought captive to the obedience of Jesus.[1] We don't look to our obedience to calm our fears. We look to His! Through His faith and obedience He has received the New Covenant. We are in Christ. Because we are in Him, we are joint heirs. We participate in the promises that He received.

How the New Covenant Works

One major provision of the New Covenant is protection. The word *saved* comes from the Greek word *sozo*. This is a comprehensive word that means to be born again, healed, delivered, blessed, prospered, set apart, made whole, *protected*, etc. This word *saved* actually speaks of everything Jesus gave us by His death, burial, and resurrection.

Protection from the devil is an essential element for living in the peace of God. Because we are hid in Him, we are protected from the evil one. However, we participate in that protection, as well as in every other benefit, by faith. Faith believes that we are in Christ and that Christ qualifies us for the inheritance.[2] Faith believes that Jesus has all authority.

---

1. See 2 Corinthians 10:5.
2. See Colossians 1:12.

Faith believes that the finished work of Jesus is sufficient to provide us with supernatural protection.

The commonly accepted belief of the church today implies that I have protection only as long as I do everything right. This is an Old Covenant concept. Unfortunately, we have tried to understand and interpret the New Covenant from the Old. If we accept the terms of the Old Covenant we have, by default, rejected the terms of the New Covenant. If that is the case, we should obey every commandment and not fail at any of them. *"For whosoever shall keep the whole law, and yet offend in one point, he is guilty of all"* (James 2:10). If our hope of any of the promises is based on our performance, we must commit to a life of flawless perfection. If we could attain to such a lofty goal, we would not, however, need Jesus as our Savior!

This concept teaches that when we fall short, we give the devil the right to work in our lives. The word *right* is synonymous with authority. The right to do anything means we have the authority to do it. So we are saying, then, that our failures give authority to the devil. Although this reasoning is completely logical, it is inconsistent with the New Covenant.

Authority does not belong to us; it belongs to Jesus.

We cannot give what is not ours. Authority does not belong to us. When Jesus arose from the dead He said, *"All authority has been given to Me in heaven and on earth"* (Matthew 28:18 NKJV). We assume that Jesus continued to say, "Now I am giving you the authority." No! He told us to use His authority. He told us to act boldly in His name. We are to act within the scope of the authority that He obtained. But never did He say that He had transferred that authority to us. It is not ours to give or lose.

Jesus did not arise from the dead and say He had some authority. He did not say He had authority until we sinned. He said, "All authority is Mine!" For us to consider that we could give authority to the devil is tantamount to usurping the Lordship of Jesus.

Jesus' mission was a success. He conquered the devil. He arose with all authority. The devil no longer has the right or the opportunity to accuse men before God. If you sin, repent. Deal with your sin. Go to God and get the help that you need, but know that your sin has not broken the covenant God made with Jesus. He is still Lord!

CHAPTER 11

SAFE IN JESUS

There were two main influences that sought to erode the doctrine of the early church. One of those was a group called the Judaizers. These were people who sought to believe in Jesus yet find a way to hold on to the teaching of Moses. They became the main influence in mixing the Old and the New Covenants. Many of Paul's epistles were written to combat the legalistic influence of this group. He recognized that mixing the covenants alienated believers from the power of God and subtly turned them to works righteousness.

The Judaizers believed that Jesus was the Messiah. They taught that you must believe on Him to be saved. But they also taught that you must obey the law to be righteous, receive the blessings, and stay saved. If you did not obey the law and maintain your righteousness by works, you lost the benefits of the New Covenant.

Nearly every book in the New Testament was written to address this error that seemed so reasonable and godly, yet rejected everything that Jesus accomplished. This concept is present and preeminent in the church today: saved by faith, righteous by works.

Paul Refuted Works Righteousness

The apostle Paul wrote the book of Colossians specifically for the purpose of refuting the erroneous teaching that when you sin you open the door to the devil and give him the right to attack you. In Colossians 2:4 Paul said, *"And this I say, lest any man should beguile you with enticing words."*

The word *beguile* means to cheat by false reckoning or deceive by false reasoning. Satan is the beguiler. He always uses something that sounds reasonable. He always starts with a truth and cunningly uses it to hide the lie. From this reasonable perspective we reason beyond reality. In so doing we cheat ourselves out of the blessing that God gave us in Jesus. While fervently seeking to take hold of truth, we let go of it as we reach out for something that fits into our carnal logic.

The most enticing logic to the human mind is works righteousness. It just makes sense to us. We can understand it! It appeals to the carnal (natural) mind. If Paul had preached works righteousness, he could have tacked Jesus onto the end of the law and he would never have been persecuted. The human mind cannot conceive of righteousness as a free gift. Rather than trusting the love of God, we trust a logic that fits our reasoning.

No one can live under the law and qualify for God's promises. The Jews tried it for a few thousand years and failed. The law states that no one will ever be justified by keeping the law. Yet, we foolishly cling to it because it fits our concept of righteousness.

Verse 6 of Colossians 2 says, *"As ye have therefore received Christ Jesus the Lord, so walk ye in him."* Keep walking in Jesus the way you came into Jesus. Since you were saved by faith, walk by faith. Verse 7 says, *"Rooted and built up in him, and stablished in the faith, as ye have been taught, abounding therein with thanksgiving."* We never grow beyond the place of trusting in the finished work of Jesus.

In verse 8 he told us the reason we have to do this. It says, "*Beware lest any man spoil you through philosophy and vain deceit, after the tradition of men, after the rudiments of the world, and not after Christ.*" The word *spoil* means to strip and to lead away captive. The Colossians had received a doctrine that is very similar to what is preached all around the world today. This doctrine came into the church by the Judaizers.

One scholar says, "The Judaizers in Colossi claimed that spirits (principalities and powers) still exercise great power and all Christians must protect themselves against it by observing rules and regulations which the Judaizers prescribed."[1] This message, though clearly refuted by the apostle Paul, is openly preached and accepted in the church today as sound doctrine.

Although the Bible obviously supports good works and godly living, it does not support a works-oriented belief system. It does not support the concept that our works righteousness provides more for us than Jesus' righteousness.

Paul strongly opposed the message of works righteousness. He taught that we should live godly, yes, but that that cannot be the basis of our faith. He also refuted the concept that Satan and his demons were powerful enough to oppose those in whom Christ dwelled. He said, "*For in him* [in Christ] *dwelleth all the fulness of the Godhead bodily*" (Colossians 2:9). In other words, everything God is and everything God has dwells in Christ Jesus. All the Godhead—Father, Son, and Holy Ghost—and everything They have dwells bodily in Christ Jesus. No demon, angel, or man has more power or authority!

---

1.   R.C.H. Lenski, *The Interpretation of St. Paul's Epistle to the Colossians, to the Thessalonians, to Timothy, to Titus and to Philemon* (Minneapolis, Minnesota: Augsburg Publishing House, 1946), p. 120.

He went on to say in verse 10, *"And ye are complete in him, which is the head of all principality and power."* The early believers were seduced into thinking the law would make them

*We are safe from the enemy because
we are in Jesus and Jesus is in us.*

complete. The logic would only follow that if the law makes me complete, it also makes me protected. However, the one thing that makes you complete, perfect, and safe from the enemy is the fact that Jesus is in you and you are in Him.

Christ in You, the Hope of Glory

This is the greatest mystery that has been hidden from the foundation of the world. This is the mystery we should proclaim, *"Christ in you, the hope of glory"* (Colossians 1:27). This truth boggles the mind that trusts in the logic of the law. My works are not the hope of my glory. Nothing is a suitable substitute for Jesus. I don't need anything else to make me complete. Christ in me is the hope of glory.

Because you are in Him, you are the one who is above all principality. The book of Colossians begins in the first chapter by stating that Jesus created everything. It says He created all principalities and powers. Before they fell He was superior to them. He is certainly superior to them now.

Paul began this letter by establishing Christ's supremacy over all created things. He showed Him as supreme authority. The terms *principalities and powers* do not necessarily refer to the demons themselves. The word *principality* basically means position or rank. The word *power* comes from the Greek word that we know as authority. Jesus created everything, including all the positions, ranks, and authority. Because He created them, He is far superior to them. Paul wanted us to be fully aware that principalities and powers are no rival for Christ Jesus the Creator.

In chapter 1 verse 20, Paul continued this systematic logic and explained that God made peace with us through the blood of Jesus. So we see that Jesus was the Creator of all principality and power. His position is supreme. We are complete in this same Person who is superior to all principality and power. God made peace with us through Him. We have been fully reconciled to God. Christ in us is the hope of the glory. From this thought Paul warned us not to allow ourselves to be beguiled.

The Colossians were beguiled in many ways. They were beguiled about what would make them complete. Few Christians ever grasp this paradox. Your works are valuable on the horizontal plane of life. Your works are an important factor in relating to this world. Yet, your works will not make you complete; Jesus did that. Your works should flow from the reality that you are complete. They should never flow from an attempt to be made complete.

*You do good works because you **are** complete,
not because you are trying to be complete.*

Your works may keep you from making serious mistakes that put you in a position of hardship. But your works can never give Satan any rights in your life. Your unbelief that springs from personal guilt can give Satan an opportunity, but it can never give him the right.

Paul warned us not to let anyone deceive us with all the teachings concerning principalities and powers. Do not believe you can give them the right to attack you. You must realize you are complete in Jesus. Because He is in you, that means the fullness of God is in you. You are safe in Jesus!

CHAPTER 12

FREE FROM ACCUSATION

In the New Covenant God removed Satan's basis for accusation against mankind. We could not experience the abundant life if we were constantly bombarded with a barrage of condemnation that kept us in continual fear.

For some it is a great mystery why and how God stopped using the law in His relationship to man. The law was given for our good, until salvation could sent. It served many positive functions. In the heart of sinful men, however, it became a destructive force that worked against us.

Jesus fulfilled all the righteous requirements of the law. He obeyed every word. This qualified Him to be the author of our salvation and the recipient of a New Covenant. Through the process of His death, burial, and resurrection, He ended the covenant based on the law. He obtained righteousness and gave it to man as a free gift. Once the covenant of the law was ended, Satan could no longer use our failure to uphold it against us.

In verse 14 of Colossians 2 Paul explained how God did this: "*Blotting out the handwriting of ordinances that was against us, which was contrary to us, and took it out of the way, nailing it to his cross.*" We have a mentality of Jesus nailing our sins to the cross. That is not, however, what He nailed to the cross.

Jesus became your sins, took the punishment for your sins, and went to Hades.

It was not your sin that Jesus nailed to the cross. He bore your sins to the grave. It was the law that He nailed to the cross. The law was the handwriting of the ordinances that stood against us. "*By the law is the knowledge of sin*" (Romans 3:20). "*The strength of sin is the law*" (1 Corinthians 15:56).

It was not our sins that Jesus nailed to the cross; it was the law.

"*Where no law is, there is no transgression*" (Romans 4:15). A new covenant had to be put into effect so that man could live at peace with himself and his God!

Jesus Stripped the Enemy

It is not insignificant to emphasize that Jesus nailed the law to the cross especially when you read the next verse in Colossians 2. Verse 15 says, "*And having spoiled principalities and powers, he made a show of them openly, triumphing over them in it.*" Paul warned earlier in this letter against the danger of being spoiled. The Scriptures said not to let a man spoil you, strip you, and lead you away captive. It was not man that was spoiled at the cross; it was all principality and power. That is right—Jesus spoiled them all. He stripped them and led them away captive. But, what did He strip from them? Whatever it was, it exposed them for what they really are.

Jesus was the Creator of all position, rank, and right (principality and power). Before Satan and his angels fell, they seemed to exist in ranks and were given authority to serve and operate in planet Earth. And there was something that gave them the opportunity to work in the life of mankind. Whatever that something was, Jesus stripped them of it and made a show of them openly.

The first thing Jesus stripped from those fallen angels was their rank, their position. Their realm was at one time very orderly. At the cross, however, all that ended. They lost their position in the spirit world. He stripped principality or rank and position. Their orderly realm never was their kingdom. They were servants of the Most High God. They only existed in rank and right because He deemed it. But at the cross that was all lost. Satan's realm is not the orderly, well-managed kingdom we had once thought. That simply is another lie behind something that was once true. Then, and most essential for mankind, Jesus stripped them of the law, that is, the handwriting of the ordinances that were against us.

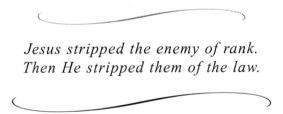

Jesus stripped the enemy of rank.
Then He stripped them of the law.

Prior to the cross the devil had one tool to use against mankind: the handwriting of the ordinances. The law was never intended to be against us. Due to the weakness of the flesh, however, we could not uphold the law and its requirements. The law was essential. It prepared the way for the Messiah. It was God's wisdom for functioning in planet Earth. But it could not make us righteous.

Satan is the accuser of the brethren. The law gave Satan the basis to accuse the brethren. As long as he had a basis to point out your failures, he had a right to accuse you. As long as he had rank and right, he had access to God to make accusation.

The Removal of the Law

Jesus had to remove the basis for accusation. Romans 4:15 points out, "*The law worketh wrath: for where no law is, there is no transgression.*" The only way to remove the basis of accusation was to remove the opportunity for transgression. The only way there could be no transgression was to remove the Old Covenant and replace it with one that provided righteousness as a free gift.

In 2 Corinthians 3:14 you will find that the removal of the law made us able to see things clearly. It made us able to see both God and the devil as they really are. The Bible says that the law was a veil over the eyes of those who were under that covenant. The veil being taken away made it possible to see God as He is and to be transformed from glory to glory.

When the law was removed, we also were able to see Satan as he is. We were able to see that he is not the leader of an organized kingdom. He is fallen. He has no rank or rights. He is little more than a gossiping liar whose only real tool against us was the law. Now that he no longer has that, he has no power over us. He would only have a basis of accusation and condemnation if we were still trying to be made righteous by the law.

Accepting Jesus as our righteousness brings the law into perspective. We can see it as wisdom from God, but we are free from our vain attempts to find righteousness in its commandments. We find our righteousness in Jesus.

CHAPTER 13

A Total Victory

The dualist view of the devil presents him nearly as powerful as God. It pictures a neck-and-neck battle that is constantly being waged for the souls of man. This unrealistic picture over-exaggerates the power of the devil and instills fear in the hearts of man. It diminishes the greatness of God, undermining our faith. It denies the cross, robbing us of our total victory over the devil.

Colossians 2:15 says that after Jesus stripped principalities and powers, He made an open show of them. The terminology in this scripture describes a specific kind of military victory. It is called a "triumphal procession." A triumphal procession only occurred when there was an absolute victory.

If you went to war, fought a battle, and had a partial victory, you did not come home and have a triumphal procession. You may have won the battle. You may have driven the armies away, but there was no triumphal procession. There may be a victory celebration of some type, but not a triumphal procession. You had won the battle, but not the war.

In a partial victory there will still be an enemy king out there somewhere. He will reassemble his armies. He will return again. His armies will still steal, kill, and destroy. The people of your kingdom will not be completely safe until there is an absolute victory. That total victory will be celebrated with a triumphal procession.

Did Jesus Win a Battle or the War?

We must determine if we believe that Jesus won an absolute victory or only a partial victory. Modern theology obviously holds that Jesus only won the battle and that we, through our works, must win the war. We have glorified the devil and trivialized the work of the cross. We have assumed the role of attaining righteousness, protection, and salvation in lieu of Jesus' limited victory at the cross. Today, however, you must see the cross as it was. You must acknowledge Jesus' total victory. His finished work must become the basis of your faith.

When a king went to battle and had an absolute victory, he returned with a triumphal procession. If he and his army killed the opposing king, they brought his head or body back. They wanted their subjects to see their enemy conquered. They wanted to remove all fear of the enemy and instill absolute confidence in their king. If the enemy king was captured, he was paraded before the citizens of the winning king.

Jesus' finished work must become the basis of our faith.

The worst thing that could happen to a king was to be captured. The torture and humiliation were unbearable. That is why King Saul killed himself rather than suffer the humiliation and torture of captivity. When an enemy king was captured, the winning side often cut off his thumbs and his big toes. This meant he could never again hold a sword or stand up in battle. They would strip him down to humiliation. They would march him, his soldiers, and all the spoil through the town as a trophy.

The conquering king sat on his horse and often dragged his enemy behind him as he rode. The women and children would spit on the enemy and beat him with rocks and sticks as he was dragged past. No one was afraid of that enemy king anymore. They were able to see him as a totally vanquished foe.

When there was a triumphal procession, it meant one thing: Never again will this enemy have the power to rise up against you. Never again will he raid our cities and villages. Never again will he hurt our children and destroy our lives. Never again will we huddle in our beds fearing his attack. He may be alive and he may even escape, but he will never again make the nations tremble.

Jesus Paraded Satan Stripped and Defeated

The Bible says that Jesus led a triumphal procession, having stripped Satan of the law. This is the equivalent to cutting off his thumbs and toes. He cannot even hold a weapon. He growls like a lion, but he is not the lion. Jesus is the Lion of the tribe of Judah. He is the real thing. Satan is the impostor. He has been stripped, humiliated, and defeated.

That is what it is talking about in Ephesians 4:8 when it says, *"He led captivity captive."* He took over and led an open procession of a defeated foe, and that procession guaranteed you and me that there would never be a time we would have to go to battle against that foe.

Unfortunately, we do not understand that the war is over. We do not realize that our enemy, although alive, has been incapacitated. He will never hold a sword and stand up against me face to face. He may spread some rumors and try to tell me lies about God. But why should I believe him, unless I missed the parade?

The war is over. We do not have to fight a defeated foe!

We are like the person who lived outside the city walls and, even though there had been a triumphal procession through the city, we were not there. We are still hiding in the hut at night afraid to go out because the enemy that was out there for so long might be waiting for us. We did not see the enemy stripped and defeated. We still view him as strong and powerful. The problem is, this powerful enemy exists only in our minds. Our misbeliefs concerning the finished work of Jesus is the breeding ground for our fears.

But now, we can see Satan as he is. All of our fear can be alleviated. Our King has won. He has emerged triumphantly with the keys of death and hell.[1] He has destroyed the works of the devil. He is King of all kings. He is the Lord of all lords. He is the Lord Triumphant!

I remember coming to this realization thirty years ago. I stood up and declared aloud, "Satan, you are a defeated foe. I will never fear you again. The battle is over!" From that moment on I have embraced the total victory of Jesus and lived free from fear of the devil! Declare your victory and end the fear!

---

1. See Revelation 1:18.

CHAPTER 14

THE PERFECT SETUP

In Paul's first letter to the Corinthians, he wrote important instructions for avoiding the trap of the devil. The Word of God is a series of instructions to show us how we can participate in the abundant life of God. Paul had written the first letter to the Corinthians to instruct them. He then followed up with another letter. It says in 2 Corinthians 2:9-11, *"I wrote to you as I did so that I could find out how far you would go in obeying me. When you forgive anyone, I do too. And whatever I have forgiven (to the extent that this affected me too) has been by Christ's authority, and for your good. A further reason for forgiveness is to keep from being outsmarted by Satan; for we know what he is trying to do"* (TLB).

Paul presented unforgiveness as a state of mind that makes it possible for Satan to outsmart us. He explained, *"we know what he is trying to do."* Unfortunately, our present paradigm of Satan has blinded us to his strategies. The church may often know what he is trying to do, but rarely do we know how he will do it. We do not understand his strategies. It is not enough to know who our enemy is and what he desires to do. To maintain victory we must know his strategies.

The issue is not one of authority and power, but of understanding. I cannot let him outsmart me. Obviously, knowing and believing the truth about the finished work of Jesus is the first and most important understanding that will maintain our victory. The next most important truth is our identity in Jesus. The third aspect of maintaining victory, however, is not a matter of active believing; it is a matter of staying clear-minded, lest we be deceived.

Recognize Satan's Strategy

Unforgiveness, like all sin, is not something that gives the devil the right to work in our lives. Lawbreakers don't look for the right; they look for the opportunity! And that's what sin gives to Satan. Now, sin does not make God stop loving and protecting us. It is, however, something that blinds us to reality. Sin always affects the soul; that is, it affects our mental and emotional capabilities. Sin perverts our perception of God, the devil, our identity, and every other reality of life and relationship. Sin is the tool that shuts our eyes to destruction and pain. It closes our ears to the voice of God that is trying to lead us into life. It hardens our heart, thereby making it difficult to feel God. It creates an opportunity for destruction.

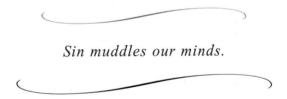

Sin muddles our minds.

It is one thing to have an enemy that wants to talk badly about you, but it is not likely you will be too concerned about this enemy. You will not prepare your defense. You will not lay awake at night jumping at every sound. But if you have an enemy that wants to kill you, that is another story. Could you imagine what it would be like if you testified against a mass murderer who had killed dozens of people? Everyone who had opposed him was found murdered, but you were assured of complete protection if you would testify.

The police said, "Do not worry. If you will testify against this guy, we will put him away. He will be in prison for life. You have nothing to worry about. You will be safe." So you reluctantly agree, "Okay, I will do it." You go to court and testify against this brutal murderer. He is sentenced to prison and it all seems to be over. The next day, however, you hear that he has escaped. How well would you sleep? How casual would you be? You would not rest until you developed a strategy with which to protect yourself and your family.

When you have an enemy, a major part of defending yourself is in knowing his strategy. The generals in charge of our armed forces study their opponents to learn their tactics. They study their mentality, the way they think, and the way they do battle. If they ever go to war, they want to know the tactics of their enemy. If you know the tactics of your enemy, you can outsmart him. The church does not seem to know the tactics of the devil. The church is extremely ignorant about his devices. Because of this, we continually fall into his hands.

Let's Change Our Strategy

We are waging a war! Unfortunately, our strategy is based on myth, tradition, and superstition. We are like a man who goes into battle blind. We hear our enemy. We know his presence. We are consumed with fear. We know he is there and wield our sword mightily in every direction, but it is futile. Our attempts are without consequence. We are like the shadow boxer Paul referred to. We simply beat the air.

We go back to the Word of God and read the passages about the battle, yet never change our paradigm. We keep going back to the battle, but each time we return a little more discouraged and worn. We are so drunk on tradition and myth that we do not seem to realize that we must change our strategy if we are to get different results. Only a fool continues to do the same things expecting to achieve different results. Let's get a new strategy!

We have sufficiently proven that Satan is not the great mastermind we had once believed. He is not as wise and strategic as we had thought. He has no authority or power. What I must learn is how I get "set up for the fall." What is it that puts me in a position for destruction?

Ephesians 4:25-27 says, *"Stop lying to each other; tell the truth, for we are parts of each other and when we lie to each other we are hurting ourselves. If you are angry, don't sin by nursing your grudge. Don't let the sun go down with you still angry—get over it quickly; for when you are angry you give a mighty foothold to the devil"* (TLB). The *King James Version* says, in verse 27, *"Neither give place to the devil."* Satan is not the great mastermind that we thought he was. Satan is not a super genius who is able to outwit and outsmart people. He simply seizes the opportunities that we give him.

Satan is not a super genius. He simply takes advantage of opportunities.

Jesus has won an absolute victory. I don't have to fight the devil to stay free from his traps. All I have to do is stop giving him the opportunity. The first step in ending his opportunity is knowing the truth. The second is living free from the blinding effects of sin.

I always taught my children to avoid places and situations that would be a setup to get robbed, mugged, or hurt. Don't park on the dark side of the mall. Don't go to certain places alone. In other words, don't get set up! You will never be set up again because now you are aware of the devil's limitations and strategies!

CHAPTER 15

ALTERED STATES

Satan is a fallen fool who has some strategies, but he can only use those strategies when we are in a wrong frame of mind. According to Ephesians, when we become angry, we are in a frame of mind that gives opportunity to the devil. Of course, anger is only one example. There are many other attitudes and emotions that make us vulnerable. Any state of mind that promotes irrationally viewing the facts will prevent us from realizing and acting on truth.

Philippians 4:5 says, *"Let your moderation be known unto all men."* Moderation is important in every area of life. Extreme emotions are blinding. Extreme euphoria is just as blinding as extreme depression. They both alter our perception of life. Extreme cravings are blinding. Esau sold his birthright for a morsel of bread. Men have sold their souls for food when hungry. Others have sold their souls for sin when lonely. The concept of moderation is essential for understanding the following verse. Luke 21:34 says, *"Take heed to yourselves, lest at any time your hearts be overcharged with surfeiting, and drunkenness, and cares of this life, and so that day come upon you unawares."* This verse warns us against any altered state that would make us unaware.

The Bible has a lot more to say about being drunk emotionally than it does about alcoholic intoxication. Being drunk physically will alter your emotions, giving opportunity to all manner of sin. The sin of getting drunk is not just because it is alcohol; it is the effect it has on your mind, perception, and judgment. Anytime you are not sober minded, you are in a position to be captured.

Anytime you are not sober minded,
you are in a position to be captured.

You are drunk when emotions and perceptions become distorted and exaggerated. Some are drunk with greed, some with lust, some with anger, and some with power. When you are drunk emotionally, the altered state makes you vulnerable. The Bible warns not to get drunk with the cares of this life so that day will not "take you unaware." The "day" is any day of trouble. You do not want to walk through life unable to clearly see and perceive trouble approaching. Therefore, verse 36 of Luke 21 says, "*Watch ye therefore, and pray....*"

Be Vigilant

The Bible tells us to be vigilant. A vigilant person, as opposed to the slothful person, is attentive to his surroundings. When you get caught up in selfish ambitions, selfish desires, lust, greed, and all other self-centered emotions, you are not attentive to what is going on around you. You have your attention focused on one thing: meeting your needs. Whenever you have your attention focused inward, you cannot see outward.

You have never lost a battle because the devil was smart. You have never lost a battle because the devil was powerful. You lost battles because you were not paying attention. You had your attention focused on some self-centered thing and you were unable to recognize what was happening to you. The devil took you unaware. He seized an opportunity that you created!

In Matthew 26:41, Jesus told the disciples to *"watch and pray, lest you enter into temptation"* (NKJV). This is speaking of vigilance in prayer and life. Prayer should be a place where we become aware of the true nature of every circumstance. Nothing should take us unaware. While we close our physical eyes to pray, we should open the eyes of our hearts to see what God is showing us about our situation.

When Gideon's army knelt at the water hole to drink, those who lapped like dogs were sent home. Those who cupped their hands and drew the water to their mouths won the battle. They represent those who, while being nourished in the Lord, continue to watch. They cannot be taken by surprise. They are vigilant!

Let's say that I am forced into a boxing match with the heavyweight champion of the world. The day comes for the big fight. I know I don't stand a chance. So I put together a strategy. Maybe I would arrange to run into my opponent just before the fight to take him out for dinner. We are eating and I ask, "Wouldn't you like to have a drink with your meal?" He is not worried because he is only going to be fighting me, so he says he will take a drink with his meal. I have the waiter pour up a long, tall drink. When the drink is gone, I ask him if he wants another one.

My goal is to get him drunk. Even though he is bigger and stronger, if I could get him drunk enough, I could beat him. I would not beat him based on my strength or ability. I would beat him based on his lack of ability at that moment. I would get him in an altered state and seize the opportunity. This is what the devil does to the believer. He simply waits until we are drunk with the cares of this life. Then he attacks! We never see it coming.

We have all authority in the name of Jesus. There is really nothing we should fear! Yet, we get drunk and lose to our enemy. Although we have the power available to us and the right or authority to use that power, because we are intoxicated emotionally we do not function the way we should. So, our enemy seizes upon our condition and beats us. The sad thing is the theology we create to explain why we were beaten. This "circumstance theology" then becomes the tradition the church accepts and passes on as reality.

*The devil simply waits until we are drunk
with the cares of this life. Then he attacks.*

Like Job, we would rather develop a doctrine that makes God responsible than ourselves responsible. In Job 34:17 God asked Job, *"Wilt thou condemn him that is most just?"* Job did not want to accept his responsibility for his predicament. He wanted to attribute his circumstance to some strange test of God. God later told him he had darkened his counsel through his words without knowledge. Job's "circumstance theology" held him in defeat until he saw it all as it really was.

Be Consumed With God, Not Desire

Satan is an opportunist, a con man. A con artist is completely dependent on the greed of his target. Unless the target gets into greed, he will see the obvious trap that is being laid for him. Everyone else sees it, but his greed closes his eyes. He cannot see beyond his sin. Similarly, in our altered states we are blinded to the obvious. We are blinded to a weak, defeated enemy that we could easily conquer.

Temptation starts from desire. James 1:14 says, "*Every man is tempted, when he is drawn away of his own lust, and enticed.*" Temptation does not start with the devil. Temptation starts with me. It starts with my desires. Remember that no desire is evil within itself. So where does the desire become evil? The desire becomes evil when we turn to any source other than God to fulfill the desire. That is when we choose sin as an option to fulfill our desire. We don't need to do that; every desire can be fulfilled in a godly, biblical manner.

When we do not believe that God will bring us fulfillment, however, we become consumed with the desire. In this state of blindness we fall into the trap of sin. Our desire, coupled with our unbelief, is the altered state that causes us to fall to a defeated foe!

Second Peter 1:4 tells us that we escape the corruption that is in the world, which comes through our desires, by the great promises God has given us in Jesus. When I know God will bring me to the fulfillment of every desire, I will not become consumed by my desire; I will be consumed with God. Then I don't have to fight with the devil. I don't have to be afraid of the devil. I simply have to trust God's great provision, and I never become vulnerable!

CHAPTER 16

PROVOKED BY INSECURITY

There are many unanswered questions about the dynamics of demonic activity and how Satan's strategies work. Unfortunately, in the absence of absolute information, we have assumed and extrapolated a doctrinal position that is not clearly supported by the Scriptures. Yet, Paul in 2 Corinthians 2:11, after warning about the problem of unforgiveness, indicated that we should be aware of Satan's devices. *"Lest Satan should get an advantage of us: for we are not ignorant of his devices."*

Maybe we have overcomplicated the devices of the devil through our over-exaggeration of his powers. Identifying what happens in the process of temptation and demonic "possession" is not difficult. Observation provides us with that data. However, we only see what happens on the outside. We do not see the subtle and often hidden internal workings of the heart.

Instead of leaping to unrealistic assumptions, why not simply look at what we know about the devil? There are only a few direct references about Satan. After examining each reference, understanding his strategy is not so difficult. His tactics may vary. There may be some circumstantial twists. There will be some overlap. But in the end, we realize that Satan's strategies are quite limited and unimaginative.

As we have previously established, Satan is an opportunist. In order for his limited strategies to succeed, we must provide him opportunity in the form of selfish, sinful motives

In the end, Satan's strategies
are quite limited and unimaginative.

and attitudes that propel us into blindness. Apart from the opportunities we create, Satan has no avenue to mankind. Therefore, the questions we must ask in our own dealings with temptation are these: "What is it I desire and do not believe God will do? What am I looking for, apart from God, for fulfillment?" When we answer these questions, we find the opportunity we have given to the devil.

Satan Enticed David

First Chronicles 21:1 says that Satan stood up against Israel and provoked David to number the nation. The law disallowed a king to number the people except for certain situations, such as when a census was taken or a special offering was to be given. David's failure to obey this scripture indicates that he was in some way failing to acknowledge God in this situation. Even Joab, one of his generals, tried to talk him out of such an action. There was something David needed that he did not trust God to provide.

I do not understand all the reasons for why God did not want the people to be numbered. However, the first thing that comes to mind would raise the question of trust. God had won battles through many and few. He wanted the leaders to trust the power and might of the God of Israel. It was essential that David keep his trust in God for security of the nation of Israel.

The word *provoked* means to seduce, entice, and persuade. We know that enticement comes when we have a desire. The desire itself is not wrong, but the enticement to fulfill it in an unbiblical manner is what leads us to sin. Desire entices, while unbelief leads us to sources other than God.

David may have wanted security from the threat of war. If so, he should have found that in God instead of in the strength of his army. He may have been facing a time of insecurity. Then he should have encouraged himself in the Lord as he did at Ziklag. Whatever the situation, David violated the Scriptures because he was enticed to act independently of God.

Satan Tempted Jesus to No Avail

When Jesus faced temptation, He modeled how it should be handled. Matthew 4:1 says, *"Then was Jesus led up of the Spirit into the wilderness to be tempted of the devil."* The word tempted literally means "tested, tried, scrutinized or proved." James 1:13 begins, *"Let no man say when he is tempted, I am tempted of God."* The Spirit of God may have led Jesus into the wilderness to seek God unless, however, the Scriptures contradict themselves. He was not led there for the purpose of temptation. He went there to prepare for His launch into public ministry!

Contrary to popular opinion, God does not test men with difficult circumstances. Neither does He put men in situations to be tempted with evil. *"God cannot be tempted with evil, neither tempteth he any man"* (James 1:13b). Man's only test is the test of faith. The test of faith is simply a matter of God's making us promises and our determining if we will believe those promises. The promises are not given to see what we will do. They are given so we will know what God will do.

The promises of God are given
*so we will know what **God** will do.*

At this point in time Jesus was beginning His public ministry. He was motivated by a godly desire, yet He faced difficult circumstances. He was preparing to declare to the world that He was the Messiah. Just imagine what a step of faith that had to be!

After fasting for forty days it was natural to desire food. This innocuous desire provided an opportunity for the enemy. Jesus was tempted to turn bread into stones. At first glance this seems harmless enough. Yet, there was something happening at a much deeper level. This temptation was cloaked in the question, "If Thou be." Satan tried to provoke Jesus into proving His identity by working miracles instead of trusting God. After all, He was hungry and He was *supposed* to be the Messiah.

Unlike David, Jesus did not succumb to the feelings of lack and insecurity by violating God's Word. At the heart of every temptation there is the feeling of need, lack, and insecurity. When we, like Jesus, know who we are in relation to God, we free ourselves from the sense of lack that draws us away from God and into temptation. We free ourselves from the trap of the enemy's devices!

CHAPTER 17

VEXED AND TORMENTED

The debate about demon possession has continued since the time of Jesus. Maybe one thing that makes it unclear is the terminology. We have made the issue of possession a battle over geographic location instead of effect. It doesn't matter where the demon is located; what matters is the effect it has on the person, what makes the person vulnerable, and how to break the effect.

The word *possessed* may be better translated as "demonized." Thayer's *Greek-English Lexicon* translates it as "to be under the power of a demon."[1] As we have previously established, this can only happen for New Covenant believers when we make ourselves vulnerable. But suffice it to say that a person is demonized when the negative, destructive influences control aspects of his life.

This word *possessed* can also mean vexed. When a person is vexed, he is emotionally consumed. A person can become vexed, or emotionally consumed, with negative or positive thoughts. However, whether those thoughts are negative or positive, the results are the same. When one is emotionally consumed he is blind. His reasoning is altered by the object of his thoughts. He focuses on one thought, desire, or fear to the

---

1. Joseph Henry Thayer, *Greek-English Lexicon of the New Testament* (Grand Rapids, Michigan: Baker Book House, 1977), p. 128.

exclusion of other important information. If you were driving while consumed by a concern about work, you might run a traffic light and be killed. A demon didn't have to live in you to make that happen. Your lack of trusting God for help gave rise to consuming fears that caused you to lose you focus. The result was destruction for you and your family.

Vexation Leads to Obsession

King David is an example of a person becoming vexed by a desire. While walking on his roof he saw a beautiful woman bathing. It was not his intention to have this experience. But once he saw her, he became obsessed by what he saw. He was tormented and harassed with the picture in his head. When a person is vexed, that sight is so strong and compelling that it stimulates certain God-given desires. But the pursuit of those desires in an ungodly manner leads to sin and destruction. When a person is vexed, his emotional torment causes him to ignore all other information. He can reason and justify his every action through the incredible compelling of a strong desire. Such a person is in demonized by vexation. It doesn't matter where the demon is or if a demon is directly involved; the person is falling prey to the works of the devil.

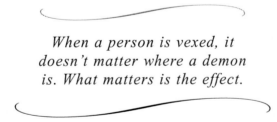

When a person is vexed, it doesn't matter where a demon is. What matters is the effect.

Lot, although a godly man, became consumed, and it nearly cost him his life. Lot's experience seems different from David's. He saw something that at first repulsed him. But he was tormented by what he saw. Second Peter 2:8 says of Lot, *"For that righteous man dwelling among them, in seeing and hearing, vexed his righteous soul from day to day with their unlawful deeds."* Lot saw and heard things that so consumed his thought life that it nearly destroyed him. We do not know if Lot was tormented by the desire to commit the sin or if he was tormented by how repulsed he had become.

Thayer's *Greek-English Lexicon* provides a more complete definition of the word *vexed*. It can mean to test by touchstone, to question by applying torture, to torture, to vex with grievous pains, to be tormented, harassed, or distressed.[2] When a person is vexed, he is obsessed by the torture, distress, and harassment that is warring in his mind. The torment can be desire, shame, disgust, anger, or any thought or emotion that dominates the mind and emotions. Jesus showed us how to use the Word of God to neutralize our torments. If we do not neutralize our torments, our life will become paralyzed—thus showing us to be demonized!

Under the Influence

In Ephesians 2:1-2, Paul gave us an astonishing revelation about the workings of the devil. *"And you He made alive, who were dead in trespasses and sins, in which you once walked according to the course of this world, according to the prince of the power of the air, the spirit who now works in the sons of disobedience"* (NKJV). When we walk in disobedience, we are under the influence of the devil, whether he is in us or not. Likewise, when we follow the course of this world, we are under the influence of the devil.

---

2. Ibid., p. 96.

Things that disgust us can vex us. Many desperate people have come to me for counseling who could not understand how they were drawn into certain temptations. One such person came to me who had accidentally walked in on two people involved in a homosexual act. She was completely disgusted and offended, yet she could not get it out of her mind. She was consumed with what she had seen.

Anything we think on becomes magnified in our thoughts. In time we become drawn to it. In a few years, she found herself committing the very act that she had seen and despised. If she had known the power of speaking the Word of God, of refocusing her thoughts on truth, she would have broken the power of vexation. Instead she was consumed until the torment became an obsession.

Anything we think on becomes
magnified in our thoughts.

We become drawn to the mental pictures we hold in our minds, whether those pictures are good or bad. I grew up hating and despising my father. As a young man I grew up vowing that I would never do the things he did. But I held that picture of my father in my mind. One day while I was in a drunken fit of rage, the girl I was with said the words I thought I would never hear: "You are just like your father." My hatred for my father vexed my mind. The obsession led me to the behavior I despised.

The real freedom from any vexation is truth. I need to believe the truth in my heart about me in Jesus. I must accept the finished work of Jesus. I must resist the doctrines that make me think the devil has power over me. I must fully commit myself to the fact that God will fulfill every desire in a godly, non-destructive manner. I do not have to sin to be fulfilled.

When vexation comes, the real question is not, "Do I need to cast the devil out of me?" The real question is, "Will I walk in the Word of God? Will I submit to the Lordship of Jesus?" It is walking in and applying the principles of the world that lead me to destruction. Therefore, I will find freedom by trusting and submitting wholeheartedly to God.

CHAPTER 18

GOD IS NOT YOUR PROBLEM

In Matthew 13:39 Jesus explained a parable about an enemy who sowed tares among the wheat. Keep in mind that tares look just like wheat, except they do not bear fruit. If we view our hearts as the earth and the wheat as the Word of God, then tares would be beliefs that are not actually consistent with the Word of God. They sound godly and they have a righteous ring to them, but in the end they do not bear fruit.

Christians are easily influenced in their beliefs. Unfortunately, we base our beliefs on the power of persuasion. The persuasiveness of the one presenting the message usually determines if we accept it. We tend to be dichotomy thinkers; we think either or. We feel we must accept or reject a belief immediately upon hearing it. The Bible, however, gives us ways to test the belief without actually running a personal risk.

How to Test Different Beliefs

The New Testament vividly presents this in the church at Corinth. There were many believers in Corinth who rejected Paul's Gospel in favor of the teaching of Apollos. At the time they heard Apollos' message, he was preaching the baptism of John. He didn't even know that Jesus had been raised from the dead. However, he was a more eloquent speaker than Paul.

Therefore, many rejected the Gospel on the basis of a more powerful preacher.

Jesus said we could tell if something was true when we put it to work. We can only know the truth when we put it into practice and thereby experience freedom. Through the persuasion of men we accept error, it doesn't produce good fruit in our lives, and then we assume the problem is ours. Some people spend their entire lives trying to get some idealistic "gospel" to work, and it never does.

The test of doctrine is fruit. If what I believe is not working, there are only a few simple possibilities. Maybe what I believe is not true. Maybe it is true and I don't really believe it in my heart. To discover if it is truth I have to qualify it. The first place I go to qualify truth is the life of Jesus. Is this consistent with the way He treated people? Then I have to ask, Is it consistent with His message? Finally, I must judge all truth by asking, Is this consistent with what Jesus accomplished by His death, burial, and resurrection? If it denies the message of the cross, either it is untrue or I am misapplying the truth.

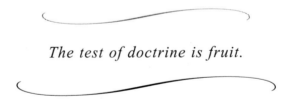

The test of doctrine is fruit.

The field of our heart is often sown with tares. We have heard things in church that are not true. We have our cultural traditions. There are plenty of opportunities to have the wind blow tares into the field of our heart. Tares grow into beliefs that look good and are logical and reasonable, but they simply do not produce good fruit. Instead, these beliefs lead us into many unproductive and destructive decisions. Like weeds in a garden, they choke out the good seed. Paul said it like this: *"A little leaven leaveneth the whole lump"* (1 Corinthians 5:6). We can't let tares grow in our hearts.

The Strategy of the Tares

One of Satan's greatest strategies is the strategy of the tares. In Mark 4:15 Jesus presented a powerful parable that expands the effects of the tares. It says, *"And these are they by the way side, where the word is sown; but when they have heard, Satan cometh immediately, and taketh away the word that was sown in their hearts."* One of Satan's major tactics is to steal the Word. He does not steal the Word because he is inside you. He does not have the ability to control your mind. Rather, he steals the Word with circumstances like affliction, persecution, cares of the world, the deceitfulness of riches, and the lust of other things.

Unfortunately, many believers confuse this strategy of the devil as a work of God. Far too many Christians think that circumstances are sent from God to test, teach, and develop our maturity. Contrary to popular thought, Jesus said that affliction, persecution, and the cares of this life will steal the Word of God from you. These things will not make you stronger; they will make you weaker.

Oftentimes people go through a difficult situation and emerge much stronger. The reason they come out stronger is because they trusted God. They saw God move on their behalf; they experienced Him as their deliverer. That which was sent to destroy them only facilitated their growth to the degree that they experienced God. Observing from the external we reason, "They were confronted with difficult circumstances and they became stronger. Since they came out stronger, God must have sent that to help them grow."

That logic is a demonic extrapolation. It is a lie hiding behind the truth. God can turn the curse into a blessing when we trust and follow Him. But He is not the source of the curse. We must know we have an enemy. He is the destroyer. God is not our tormentor. He is our comforter!

*God is not our
tormentor; Satan is!*

From this faulty belief many people have been embittered against God. After years of pain and suffering without finding the answer, they become angry with God for putting them through these hardships. At that moment, the strategy has worked. Hardships have turned us against God. Sadly, it was not really the hardships that turned us against God. It was the tares—the little misbeliefs about God. The main one is that He is the source of our trouble. God is not your problem!

CHAPTER 19

PUSHED INTO ISOLATION

W hen I was a freshman in high school, I drew a picture of a button on my notebook. Under it I wrote, "Panic button, think twice before pushing." Even though it was meant as a joke, I have thought of it often as an adult. I realize that a panic button is what you push when you want more trouble. It is always better to think than to act in haste.

In Luke 8:29 we have the account of Jesus with the demoniac. *"For he had commanded the unclean spirit to come out of the man. For oftentimes it had caught him: and he was kept bound with chains and in fetters; and he brake the bands, and was driven of the devil into the wilderness."* There are two immediate revelations from this passage. The first comes from the word *driven*, which literally means to push.

What Pushes You?

When we feel ourselves being pushed, it is usually by fear. Fear is not a tool God uses. This feeling of being pushed is facilitated by our inability to deal with circumstances, thoughts, and emotions. The sense of urgency is created in our minds. Many businesses and ministries are run in a crisis management mentality. "The squeaky wheel gets the grease" is the motto that some live and work by. But those who are driven by the pressures of the immediate are never guided by priority.

They can't follow God and His plan because of the urgency of the situation. They feel pushed into their decisions rather than led.

Unfortunately, these people fail to identify the things in life that are important and essential. They are too busy simply surviving. Or, at least they think they are surviving. The illusion of crisis living is that we must deal with the urgent. We fail to see that the urgent is not always the most important. The important and essential are always there. If it is important, it will be important tomorrow; it will be important a year from now. The urgent, however, screams out that you must do it now. It pushes you to act, regardless of your values.

Because we spend our lives and time responding to the urgent, we seldom do that which is essential and important. This type of decision-making leads to an increase in conflict, loss, and failure. Thus, we are once again destroyed. We are not destroyed by the power of the devil; we are destroyed by the lack of diligence in the essential areas of life.

If we spend our lives and time responding to the urgent, we will seldom do what is essential and important.

Your job is important, but so is your family. After years of responding to the urgencies of your job, you may find that you have neglected that which was more important. You find that you lose your family because you always responded to the pressures of work. Jesus always had people pressing Him to attend to the urgent. Instead, He continued to do what was important. He did not come when Lazarus was sick. He stuck to His priorities. He stopped along the way to help the urgent needs, but He never left the way to follow urgent needs.

When we feel pushed, we should learn to reevaluate. Think twice before you push that panic button that throws you into action. That which is urgent, pushy, or demanding is seldom coming from God. The need may be real, but that does not make it our priority.

Our faulty values and low self-worth lead us to the urgent. We feel pushed to satisfy everyone's demands. But in the end we have neglected God and the more weighty matters of life. Only allow something to become urgent in your mind if it fits into your priorities. Do not be led down paths by the priorities of others, lest you spend your life laboring for the agenda of another.

Living in Isolation

People who are being "pushed" emotionally always end up alone. Whether positionally or emotionally, the feeling of being pushed leads us to isolation. And that is the second thing that emerges about this demoniac. He was pushed into isolation. When we are pushed, we do not have time to connect with people. Even if we are doing things for people, we are seldom connecting to them. We are merely responding to the pressure of urgency.

One powerful tactic of the devil is to cut you off from people physically and emotionally. After years of working with substance abuse, codependency, and other types of serious dysfunction, I have seen that there is always social dysfunction at work. People who come out of those backgrounds have serious social issues. Those who do not develop and maintain meaningful relationships, seldom survive.

Isolation is the breeding ground for fantasy, loneliness, and all sorts of negative imaginations. When children begin to go through puberty, they often isolate themselves from other family members. They are pushed into isolation by the vexation of their desires. In this isolation they often fantasize about the new desires they feel. The isolation becomes a breeding ground for sin. Similarly, when people are ridden with shame, guilt, and obsession, they tend to isolate.

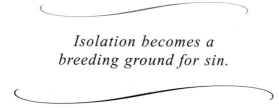

Isolation becomes a
breeding ground for sin.

We are social, emotional, and relationship-oriented beings. We are designed to function in the context of healthy relations. Although everyone wants a certain amount of time alone, isolation is a critical warning sign that we are being demonized. In this vacuum we create the opportunity for many destructive tendencies.

When you feel pushed, put on the brakes! Do not give in to the demands of the urgent. Determine what your life's priorities will be. Then live by those priorities. Do not allow the urgent to push you away from the relationships and commitments that will guide your life toward God's peace and promises!

CHAPTER 20

THE POWER OF DEATH IS BROKEN

Many people fear the devil because they believe he has the power to kill them at will. Just watch any horror movie, and you will go to bed wondering if the devil can kill you. Hebrews 2:14-15 says, *"Forasmuch then as the children are partakers of flesh and blood, he also himself likewise took part of the same; that through death he might destroy him that had the power of death, that is, the devil; and deliver them who through fear of death were all their lifetime subject to bondage."*

If Jesus has succeeded at His mission—and He did—then the devil does not have the power to take our lives. Yet, the Scriptures are clear that *"the thief cometh not, but for to steal, and to kill, and to destroy"* (John 10:10). While he has no rights and no power to accomplish this goal, he still plays a part in accomplishing this feat. "How," you may ask, "can Satan do this with no power and authority?"

Yielding to the Wrong Influence

Ananias and Sapphira present a unique insight into Satan's accomplishing the perfect snare. Acts 5:3 says, *"But Peter said, Ananias, why hath Satan filled thine heart to lie to the Holy Ghost, and to keep back part of the price of the land?"* The word *filled* is the same word that is used to describe the influence of the Holy Spirit in our lives. The word *filled* is not talking about a physical measure as much as it refers to an emotional influence.

To be filled means to "yield to the influence." When we are filled with the Holy Spirit, we are yielding to the influence of the Holy Spirit in our hearts. We see this comparison drawn in Ephesians 5:18 where it says, "*Be not drunk with wine, wherein is excess; but be filled with the Spirit.*" Being drunk is a result of being under the influence. Likewise, being filled with the Holy Spirit is being under the influence of the Holy Spirit. Yet, we must yield to the influences of the heart by choice. They cannot be forced upon us!

Just as we can yield to the influence of the Holy Spirit, so we also can yield to the influence of Satan. This is precisely what happened to Ananias and Sapphira. They yielded to the influence. Some people think Satan killed this couple. Still others believe God killed them for lying to the Holy Spirit. But the original language reveals something quite different.

Acts 5:5 tells us that hearing these words so affected his heart that Ananias and then his wife died on the spot. "*Then Ananias, hearing these words, fell down and breathed his last*" (NKJV). The Greek language is very clear that Ananias was not acted upon by an outside source. Neither God nor the devil killed him. He died as a result of his own beliefs.

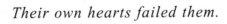

Their own hearts failed them.

Satan cannot kill you, but *you* can kill you. Ananias was fresh out of the law, the tool that Satan still uses to instill fear in the hearts of man through guilt and condemnation. This couple did not know that there was mercy and forgiveness for any sin. The church was in its infancy. Paul had not yet written

Wow!

his epistles about faith righteousness and our identity in Jesus. They came from a belief system that required death for blasphemy. Their heart was full of tares.

Satan was the influence they were yielding to in their hearts. When Peter presented a word of knowledge and confronted them with their sin, they could have repented and dealt with the issue. If their hearts had been yielded to the influence of the Holy Spirit, that is exactly what would have happened. Instead Satan, the accuser of the brethren, influenced them and they yielded. Their own hearts failed them because of the fear generated by their beliefs.

Much cutting-edge research indicates that every cell in the body knows and believes everything that we believe in our hearts. The science of cloning reveals the vast amounts of knowledge in each cell of the body. If this is true, then every cell in our body will work to carry out our beliefs. Ananias and Sapphira believed they should die because of who they had yielded to in their hearts. Their bodies did the rest!

Faulty Beliefs Produce Domination

Acts 10:38 says, *"How God anointed Jesus of Nazareth with the Holy Ghost and with power: who went about doing good, and healing all that were oppressed of the devil."* The word *oppressed* means to exercise harsh control or to dominate. The devil is a harsh dominator and he will do it through people. All domination is demonic. Force cannot be used in the kingdom of God! There is no need to have a demon in you when someone can control you from without.

Domination, however, is the product of a faulty belief system. We can be dominated only when we are looking to someone to meet a need in our life, when we are fearful, or when we suffer from low self-worth. Accepting who we are in Jesus, trusting God, and making Him our source is the key to freeing ourselves from the control of others. We would, however, only yield to control and force if the beliefs of our hearts were already embracing the *"doctrines of devils"* (1 Timothy 4:1). Doctrines of devils are not doctrines that lead you into ritualistic worship of the devil. They are simply doctrines that lead you away from the finished work of Jesus.

There is no need to have a demon within when someone can control you from without.

First Thessalonians 2:18 says, *"Wherefore we would have come unto you, even I Paul, once and again; but Satan hindered us."* Satan hinders, but not by some supernatural power. He hinders through people who embrace the world's system. It was people who hindered Paul from fulfilling his ministerial plans. Evil people, who had their personal, religious agenda, hindered him by imprisonment, persecution, and opposition.

It is important to recognize that most of Paul's persecution came about because he failed to follow the direction God gave him. God sent him to the Gentiles. However, he let his passion for the Jews, the urgency of their need, adjust that priority. It was his attempt to reach the Jews first that resulted in the majority of Paul's persecution. His disobedience put him in harm's way. He could have avoided the majority of his "demonic hindrances" if he had embraced the priorities that God gave him.

The Bible says, *"Hope deferred maketh the heart sick"* (Proverbs 13:12). When you are hindered and unable to move in the direction of your dreams and goals, your heart gets sick—that is, it gets dysfunctional. Since the heart is the seat of love, faith, and all emotions, it is essential to keep a healthy heart. A sick heart is unable to trust God for the fulfillment of dreams.

A sick heart alters the way we think and feel. It affects how every cell in our body works. A sick heart will lead us to destruction and in our hearts we will blame God. Recognizing the role we play in the dynamics of demonic activity puts us in an entirely new arena. We no longer see ourselves as powerless victims standing against a powerful adversary. Instead we see Satan as he is...a hopeless, powerless liar.

CHAPTER 21

SATAN'S SECRET WEAPON

With each page you read, you should have a growing awareness of Satan's limited power. His total lack of authority should become absolutely clear. Likewise, you should have a new awareness of your personal responsibility in escaping his snares. For the first time you can possibly say, "I am not ignorant of his devices." You can be assured that he will never take you unaware.

Satan's greatest weapon, however, may not be sin itself. Rather, it may be the tool he uses to make us vulnerable to sin. It is here the immature *in the word of righteousness* stop short of absolute victory. This is the place where the controller revolts. This is the stumbling stone of the Gospel.

Satan does not sneak his most effective secret weapon into the church from the back door. A cult or the occult does not bring it to us cloaked in a shroud of darkness. It is not concocted in the dark rooms of the wicked. Instead, the children of God in nearly every pulpit proclaim it the world over. It is applauded and "Amened" every Sunday. Simply put, it is the message of works righteousness.

In an absence of confidence in God's grace, law has become the tool the church uses to keep the children of God walking the "straight and narrow." Obedience to the law offers the empty promise of righteousness. Fear of the curse of the law has been the driving force that has so blatantly replaced dependence on the Holy Spirit! Much to the dismay of leaders around the world, legalism has had the opposite effect. Instead of leading people out of sin, it has driven them deeper into sin. Instead of facilitating faith in God, it has made people run in fear from God. It has given sin and condemnation the opportunity to come alive in our members. It has dis-empowered the people of God. It has cut us off from the grace of God and made us powerless.

Our Own Works Can Trip Us

First John 5:18 says, *"We know that whosoever is born of God sinneth not."* The entire concept of staying out of sin is foreign to most. However, the first key to staying out of sin is having a fulfilled life. If you do not lack, you probably will not lust. One can only live in a state free from desire when he believes that God wants him to have all of His promises. Additionally, one must believe that in Christ he is qualified for the promises. If this were our belief system, then why would we sin? If I have everything I need that pertains to life and godliness, it will be easy to keep myself free from the snares of the world. The world has nothing to offer the man who has everything!

The verse goes on to say, *"He that is begotten of God keepeth himself, and that wicked one toucheth him not."* This is one of the most ignored Scripture passages in the Bible. I have had people become extremely angry with me for even quoting it. The idea of this much personal responsibility may be more than some can bear.

This verse tells me that if I know how to "keep myself," the wicked one cannot touch me. When I wrote *The Prayer Organizer* and it first began to sell across America, I received many angry letters from people for having this verse included in the text. Those who had lost loved ones to death, disease, and disaster felt this to be a challenge to the righteousness of those people.

The letters of rebuke would usually make some reference to a friend or loved one who "deserved to be healed as much as anyone." This mind-set proves my position. We expect to be delivered based on our level of personal performance. We are not kept, however, because of the quality of our personal righteousness. We are kept by faith in His righteousness. Our protection is based on our faith in Jesus' finished work, not our works.

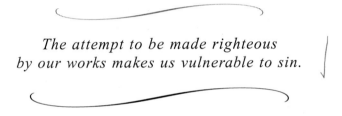

The attempt to be made righteous by our works makes us vulnerable to sin.

Death and destruction work through sin. Sin works through the law. *"O death, where is thy sting? O grave, where is thy victory? The sting of death is sin; and* **the strength of sin is the law.** *But thanks be to God, which giveth us the victory through our Lord Jesus Christ"* (1 Corinthians 15:55-57). Apart from the law sin has no strength. It is impotent! This is obviously confusing for the carnal mind. In the natural we proclaim that the law keeps people out of sin. According to the Word of God, however, that just isn't true!

The attempt to be made righteous by our works makes us vulnerable to sin. Works righteousness alienates us from the grace of God, which empowers us to live in righteousness. Sin, as we have seen, provides the opportunity for Satan to draw us into destruction. Sin is empowered by our attempt to live under the law of works righteousness.

Paul made a startling statement about his personal life in Romans 7:8. *"But sin, taking occasion by the commandment, wrought in me all manner of concupiscence. For without the law sin was dead."* Paul recognized that sin had no authority over him, but that it could seize the opportunities he gave. The opportunity that he gave was returning to the law for righteousness.

Sin Uses the Law to Its Advantage

Sin has power only to the degree we are under law. It does not say "under the Law of Moses." The definite article is not present in this verse. It is not necessarily talking about the Law. It is talking about the realm of law, any law. Our laws are the products of religious, cultural traditions that we have come to accept. Every group—denominational or non-denominational—has its laws. Every group has what it believes will qualify them for the blessings of God.

The very foundation of the Gospel is repentance from dead works.[1] Dead works are not drinking, smoking dope, running wild, and committing adultery. That is sin. No! Dead works are the works you do to make yourself right with God. They are the things you do to earn the blessings of God. They are the works you trust more than the finished work of Jesus.

Paul said that sin takes occasion by the commandment, for without law sin is dead. In Romans 6:14 the Bible says, *"For sin shall not have dominion over you: for ye are not under the law."* The thing that brings the dominion of sin in your life is the law that you trust more than you trust Jesus.

---

1. See Hebrews 6:1.

Paul then described what must have been a personal struggle in his own life. *"For I was alive without the law once: but when the commandment came, sin revived, and I died"* (Romans 7:9). Paul, like all of us, experienced what it was like to be set free from sin. Paul was never alive apart from the law until he was saved. At some point in his walk with God he must have reverted back to his legalism. He had to work this issue through just as we do. I'm sure this was the process he walked through during those fourteen years of obscurity. When he had resolved these issues in his own heart, he was sent out by the Holy Spirit to take the message of grace and peace to the world.

The person living under law is always living in fear. He is facing life in his own strength. He is forever dreading the battle that will be greater than his own strength. He may talk about the power of God, but in actuality he has no concept of what it means to rest in the grace of God. All he knows is doing the best he can for God. It is a tiring daily effort to manage an endless moral inventory in hopes of pleasing a perfect God.

Freedom from law simply means that
we have righteousness apart from the law.

This person fears the devil. His entire doctrine of Satanism revolves around *his* faith, *his* works, *his* authority... *him, him, him.* Instead of Jesus being his hope and confidence, he is his only source of confidence. His confidence to stand against the devil is based on his ability to justify his actions. This type of thinking actually promotes a life of denial and self-righteousness. It is essential that this person be right in his every action. Being wrong could open the door to the devil. Sadly, he does not realize that he is complete in Jesus.

Freedom from law does not mean that we reject the values that are embodied in the law. It is not an excuse to live in ungodliness. Paul warned against this type of deception. Sin is never acceptable. But the person who sins is always acceptable. Freedom from law simply means that we have righteousness apart from the law. Our righteousness is based on the finished work of Jesus. No matter how logical it may seem, we must never reject the righteousness of God for our own righteousness.

> But now the righteousness of God without the law is manifested, being witnessed by the law and the prophets; even the righteousness of God which is by faith of Jesus Christ unto all and upon all them that believe: for there is no difference (Romans 3:21-22).

This scripture flies in the face of every legalist. But it is our only hope of confidence in the face of the accuser. When our righteousness is not based on our performance, we have no need to blame and justify. When we feel the cold hand of accusation, we simply repent with no fear of vulnerability.

No matter how sincere the intention, the person seeking righteousness by works is rejecting the righteousness of God. He is vulnerable to every accusation. He is overwhelmed by every failure! Paul said, "For they being ignorant of God's righteousness, and going about to establish their own righteousness, have not submitted themselves unto the righteousness of God. For Christ is the end of the law for righteousness to every one that believeth" (Romans 10:3-4).

Trust in the righteousness of Jesus and forever escape the most deadly of Satan's devices!

CHAPTER 22

CONDEMNATION: SPIRITUAL CANCER

Jesus died to give us the abundant life. Abundance is one of our greatest deterrents to sin. If I have all my needs met, how could I be tempted? I don't have any lack. Abundance stands in direct opposition to lack. When I am following Jesus as my shepherd, I will not lack.[1]

To participate in the abundant life I must have an emotional base of love. Our emotional base is the foundation of our emotions. It is the place from which all our emotions evolve. Therefore, the base emotion is the guiding emotion that affects and influences all other emotions.

When love is our base emotion, we will grow into every healthy, positive emotion. We could easily identify hundreds of positive emotions that naturally emerge from this base emotion. But it may be more beneficial to identify the one emotion that will always be absent when love is our base emotion—fear!

Fear has to do with torment.[2] Fear and love cannot co-exist. To the degree that we are established in and experiencing God's love, fear is driven out. It is like light and darkness. Light always drives out darkness. It is impossible to

---

1.   See Psalm 23:1.
2.   See 1 John 4:18.

experience the abundant life beyond our experience of God's incredible love.

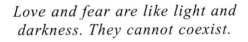

Love and fear are like light and
darkness. They cannot coexist.

Torment is the work of the devil. Contrary to commonly accepted beliefs, we do not have to be possessed of the devil to be demonized. All we have to do is embrace certain beliefs. Any belief or misbelief that robs me of the love of God causes me to be demonized. Any belief that causes me fear ushers me into a realm where I experience the effects of being demonized. Any belief that allows torment in my life has caused me to be demonized.

Once I have embraced any misbelief, I am affected on all levels of my existence. The wrong beliefs don't simply affect my relationship with God. They cause me to have emotional conflicts and dysfunction. Sickness even emerges in the opportunistic environment of negative emotions.

Guilt & Condemnation

When a person lives his life under the vain pursuits of works righteousness, the natural consequence is guilt and condemnation. Guilt and condemnation are the natural product of the law. The law does not empower for righteousness. It does not set one free. It simply makes us aware of our failures. *"By the law is the knowledge of sin"* (Romans 3:20). In fact, the law was called a ministry of condemnation.[3]

---

3.   See 2 Corinthians 3:9.

Guilt is the negative feeling we experience when we have done something wrong. Guilt is the voice of our conscience. The feeling of guilt dissipates, however, as we harden our heart. Condemnation is the expectation of judgment and punishment. Thayer's *Greek-English Lexicon* translates it as a "damnatory sentence" of judgment.[4] The person who is under condemnation expects bad things to happen. His negativity, however, exceeds the bounds of mere pessimism; he expects punishment from God for his shortcomings.

Unfortunately, condemnation finds many tormenting voices that fuel its flames. When we fall short and things go wrong in our lives, there are well-meaning people who are quick to remind us of our shortcomings. They reaffirm our fear that God is punishing or will punish us. Invariably, they will convince us that God is either punishing us or allowing the devil to punish us. The devil is often erroneously portrayed as God's tool of vengeance. If, according to the lie behind the truth, God removes His protection from us, we are defenseless against the evil one. Although this is true, it would violate the New Covenant.

If they blame the pain on God, they say He is doing it to teach us. If they blame the pain on the devil, they contend that God is allowing it. Either misbelief stands in opposition of the cross. Galatians 3:13 tells us, *"Christ has redeemed us from the curse of the law, having become a curse for us"* (NKJV). Why would God redeem us from the curse and then place the curse upon us? He would not!

Hebrews 10:26-27 has been a source of fear and torment for many who have struggled. It says, *"For if we sin wilfully*

---

4.   #G2631.

after that we have received the knowledge of the truth, there remaineth no more sacrifice for sins, but a certain fearful looking for of judgment and fiery indignation, which shall devour the adversaries." All sin, whether willful or unwillful, is the direct result of not trusting God's provision and promise. And according to Romans 14:23, what is not of faith is sin. Although all sin may not be deliberate choice, all sin is willful. We are freed from the bondage to sin. We have the freedom of choice in every situation.

These Hebrew believers had left the law to look to Jesus for relief from sin. Now that they were looking back to the law, they were rejecting the finished work of Jesus. Because Jesus is the final solution for sin, there is nowhere else to look. There is no better covenant. There are no more promises. This is the best there is. And because there is no more sacrifice for sin, we begin to expect judgment. The rationale of the legalist is based on the reality that this is what happened to those who opposed Moses and the law. It did not say that this is what we would receive; it said that this is what we begin to *expect*. This is condemnation: the expectation of judgment!

Sin is the direct result of not trusting
God's provision and promise.

The voice of doom and gloom that you hear in your mind is not the voice of God; it is the voice of condemnation. The voice of condemnation is not the devil speaking into your mind. It is your own voice speaking your misbeliefs. And as always, these misbeliefs have just enough truth to hide the lie! When we sin, the Holy Spirit does convict us. He does not, however, torment us. He is the comforter. He reminds us of the promise of God; He draws us back to God. He encourages and leads us. He reminds us that we are righteous. He points us to the cross. It is our own conscience that smites our hearts. Our conscience speaks what our heart believes! If our heart is not established in love, our heart will always speak fear and condemnation. It is our faulty beliefs that condemn us.

Sin & Judgment

Physiologically, the heart of a man will attempt to make what he believes come to pass. It has been said that the DNA—the individual and collective intelligence of the human cell—will work together to make what we believe come to pass. In other words, when you believe something at the heart level, every cell in your body works to make it come to pass.

If you expect punishment, you will experience punishment. It will not be from God, but it will be torment. Statistics show that disaster seems to strike, for most people, at the time of their greatest opportunity. Is this coincidence? No! Is this the work of the devil? Not directly! This is the work of mis-beliefs and condemnation.

Guilt says you have done something wrong; condemnation says this is your punishment. Whatever you believe your sentence to be, whatever you believe the price of your sin to be, your heart will attempt to make you pay...and every cell in your body will cooperate. For some there is the belief that they do not deserve to have love in their life. For others there is the belief that they do not deserve good things. I have known people who did not believe they deserved to be happy. Still others insist they deserve to be sick. Whatever your expectation of punishment is, your heart will work to make it come to pass.

Another subtle way condemnation works to destroy us is when our life begins to exceed what we believe we deserve. When this happens, our heart works to pull us back to the level of what we feel we deserve. This is why many people die shortly after retirement. They do not feel they deserve to live if they are not working. This is why many people self-destruct. When they have their greatest opportunities for love, happiness, and fulfillment, they have to "blow it up"! We have been demonized by our own condemnation.

Life in Christ should be the end of condemnation. *"There is therefore now no condemnation to them which are in Christ Jesus, who walk not after the flesh, but after the Spirit. For the law of the Spirit of life in Christ Jesus hath made me free from the law of sin and death"* (Romans 8:1-2). Being in the spirit is simply the belief that we are made righteous and empowered to righteousness by the Spirit of God who dwells in us. Being in the flesh is when we attempt to be made righteous by our works.

You will end the torment in your life when you embrace God's perfect love and forgiveness in Christ Jesus!

CHAPTER 23

THE TRUTH BEHIND THE LIE

Truth is simple. Our capacity to grasp truth, however, presents very real challenges. Jesus told the Pharisees, "Because you say you see, you are blind." (See John 9:41.) Insisting that we see a truth blinds us to other possibilities. Our struggles to grasp truth is largely because of the way we think. We tend to be linear thinkers. Everything is one way or another. We are not trained to think within the framework of the paradox.

Truth and reality are filled with paradoxes. One of the laws of Heart Physics® reveals that all things exist between the poles of opposites realities. Nothing in nature can exist apart from this law of physics, and neither can any truth.[1] It is essential that we grasp the paradox present in every truth; otherwise, we fail to find the reality present in the truth.

Freedom, like all truth, has a paradox. Freedom cannot exist if it is void of boundaries. One can never experience freedom beyond the level of personal responsibility. Jesus died to give us freedom—freedom from sin, freedom from works righteousness, but not freedom from boundaries. Apart from boundaries we become enslaved again.

---

1. Heart Physics is a unique work developed by Dr. Jim Richards based on Romans 1:20. All the laws of nature reveal the unseen laws of God. For more information go to www.HeartPhysics.com or call 256-536-9402.

Although our freedom in Christ is independent of works, it is not without responsibility. Satan is a defeated foe, undeniably! The battle is over; yet we have a responsibility to believe and walk in the reality that Jesus purchased. In the Old Testament God said, "The battle is Mine." Yet, people still had to go to war. The writer of Hebrews presented this paradox: "*Let us labour therefore to enter into that rest*" (Hebrews 4:11). Hence, there is a rest you can't earn but must labor to get there. Jesus' entire message presents a concept that states, "Obey Me to live in freedom." There is no reality that does not exist between seemingly opposing truths.

Freedom requires responsibility.

Responsible living is essential for maintaining victory. But we have a tendency to turn responsibility into legalism. Responsibility says, "I take this step because it is the wise thing to do. It will bring me to my goals." Legalism would say, "I take this step to get God to do something for me." The action taken is neither good nor bad. But the motive for taking the action could be the precursor to success or destruction.

Satan Merely Impersonates a Lion

We need to be clear that the devil seeks our destruction. Yet, it is equally essential that we understand his devices lest we create a strategy that promotes fear instead of faith. Satan is an impersonator. He depends on our misbelief to keep us trapped in the illusion of his power. First Peter 5:8 in the *New International Version* says, "*Be self-controlled and alert. Your enemy the devil prowls around like a roaring lion looking for someone to devour."*

Satan is looking for a way to destroy you. He is impersonating a lion, a most vicious predator. While spending time in Africa, I experienced what it was like to hear lions roaring at night. It is a frightening sound. It carried for miles. Although the lions roared all night, I slept free from fear. Why? I knew they were captive in a zoo. If I had gone into their area, they could have killed me. That would not have happened, however, because I had no freedom. I had the freedom to choose where I walked and slept. Either choice would not have changed God's love and protection for me. If, however, I had foolishly chosen to walk in the lion's den, I would have died. So it is with the devil.

The moment we remove the "fangs of the serpent," he is no longer a threat. In the case of the devil, he has already been defanged. We must simply look to the cross to see him as he really is. Then we will understand the strategies that will give us complete freedom. In an instant this revelation will highlight both our freedom and our responsibility beyond what we have previously known.

Seeing the Devil As He Really Is

Isaiah 14:16 prophesies of a day when we will experience seeing the devil as he really is: *"They that see thee shall narrowly look upon thee, and consider thee, saying, Is this the man that made the earth to tremble, that did shake kingdoms."* What a shocking and potentially embarrassing situation! In that day we will look on Satan in total disbelief and we will question, "Is he the one that made the nations tremble? Is this the one who made me cower in fear?" This startling reality will be hard to accept once we see him as he is. It will be hard to conceive how such a weak, defeated individual could have wreaked such destruction on the earth, particularly to the children of God.

There is no need, however, to wait until sometime in the future to see him in all his weakness and disarray. We need only look to the cross of Christ; the death, burial, and resurrection; the triumphal procession; the power of the resurrection; the glorious exaltation to the right hand of God signifying that it is finished. Accepting the message of the cross in its entirety will deliver us from any inflated images of Satan.

Seeing Satan as he really is comes down to our beliefs about the finished work of Jesus. To learn to spot counterfeit money, people spend more time studying real currency. You have to know the real to spot the fake. We have focused too much time on the devil without first establishing a clear-cut picture of the finished work of Jesus.

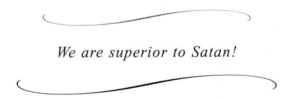

We are superior to Satan!

Satan is stripped of his power and authority. We are superior to him in every way. Our standing with God is far superior to anything he has ever known. Whose report will you believe? The truth behind the lie is not that difficult to grasp. The truth is this: Satan is a murderer. The lie is this: Satan doesn't have the power to hurt you. The truth within the paradox says: If you align yourself with this world's system, you will see destruction not by his hand or God's hand but, like Ananias in Acts 5, by your own hand. If you align your beliefs with God's reality, you are untouchable!

CHAPTER 24

SPIRITUAL WARFARE: THEN AND NOW

The mere mention of spiritual warfare immediately creates a vast array of pictures in one's mind that range from hilarious to frightening. Many believers have very strong opinions about spiritual warfare and how it should be conducted. Like any other area of strong opinion, we must be open to other possibilities before we see them.

Unfortunately, many of the concepts of spiritual warfare are based on a faulty belief about Satan. Starting from an unscriptural belief about who Satan is in turn leads us to a faulty belief about how we should deal with him.

As with every other belief we hold, our views on spiritual warfare should be scrutinized on the basis of scriptural consistency, content, and context. We must look at all our scriptures concerning warfare in light of the context in which they are written. Too often we take verses out of context and make them say something they are not saying. Too much of our doctrine concerning spiritual warfare is built on predetermined beliefs that are contradictory with the context from which we draw our references.

We must then make sure that our interpretation of those scriptures does not violate what we know about Jesus' finished work on the cross. When our interpretations violate what we know to be true of the cross, we must rethink our position.

The church world embraces far too many doctrinal positions that deny the work of the cross. This must be the acid test of all Bible doctrine.

Our present-day view of spiritual warfare is based on several faulty premises. First is an over-exaggerated concept of Satan before the fall; second is an unrealistic concept of Satan after the fall. From that faulty paradigm people look to a few Old Testament scriptures, completely ignoring the work of the cross, and develop a doctrine of warfare that is nonexistent in the New Testament.

Jesus' finished work on the cross is the acid test for all our beliefs and doctrines.

The two greatest tragedies about our warfare doctrines is that there is no consideration for the fact that Jesus rose from the dead and established a completely new covenant. There is no consideration for the complete and total victory Jesus won over Satan. It is tantamount to the denial of the death, burial, and resurrection. Secondly, there is no consideration for the context within which the New Testament warfare passages are written.

The Holy Spirit Speaks to Our Hearts

The main basis of doctrine for spiritual warfare comes from the book of Daniel. Daniel had set his heart to hear from God. He prayed and then fasted for twenty-one days until his answer came. An angelic being delivered a message to Daniel, but the prince of Persia had withstood him. Michael, the archangel, came and fought against the prince of Persia so the messenger angel could complete his mission.

> *Then said he unto me, Fear not, Daniel: for from the first day that thou didst set thine heart to understand, and to chasten thyself before thy God, thy words were heard, and I am come for thy words. But the prince of the kingdom of Persia withstood me one and twenty days: but, lo, Michael, one of the chief princes, came to help me; and I remained there with the kings of Persia* (Daniel 10:12-13).

This is a true story. It is completely valid to understand spiritual warfare from this scripture if you were alive more than 2,000 years ago. This scenario is only possible prior to the death, burial, and resurrection of Jesus. This story is completely impossible in the day in which we live.

How can I say that? For one thing, we must realize that Daniel did not have the Spirit of God living in his heart. The Old Testament believers were not born again. For this reason, God had to speak to them through external sources such as angels, prophets, and signs. It is so unfortunate to see New Testament believers seeking these Old Testament experiences. God paid a great price for the opportunity to inhabit mankind by His Spirit.

We seem to have little regard for the privilege to hear God's voice. We ignore the voice of God in our hearts in search of the voice of God in our ears. We reject the ministry of the Spirit and seek a prophet, as if his word would be surer than the word we hear in our hearts.

Hebrews 1:1 says, *"In the past God spoke to our forefathers through the prophets at many times and in various ways, but in these last days he has spoken to us by his Son"* (NIV). In the past God spoke in many different ways. Today, all He has to say is said by and through the Son. This way is better. This is what men like Daniel and Elijah longed for.

When Jesus prepared to leave planet Earth, He gave His followers their operating procedures. He let them know the means whereby God would teach and speak to them and therefore to us. *"But the Comforter, which is the Holy Ghost, whom the Father will send in my name, he shall teach you all things, and bring all things to your remembrance, whatsoever I have said unto you"* (John 14:26).

God no longer has to speak to man through angels. He has sent His Spirit to live in us; to teach, counsel, and comfort us. Therefore, no message from God can be postponed by a demon in the heavenly realm. The message will not come through the heavenly realm; it will be spoken directly into our hearts by His Spirit.

Demons in the Air Are Not the Problem

There is another assumption concerning the heavenly realms. It is assumed that these demons still hold positions in the heavenlies. The entire doctrine of hierarchy over cities revolves around one phrase: *principalities and powers*. We must remember that Jesus stripped principalities and powers and led them away captive.[1] He made a public show of them at the cross. There was a "triumphant procession" of absolute victory.

Secondly, we must realize that there is no New Testament pattern for trying to cast demons out of the air. Paul once was in a completely demonic city. The entire city was given over to idols. He did not attempt to remedy the problem by trying to cast demons out of the air; instead, he preached the Gospel to rid people of demons in their hearts.

---

1.   See Colossians 2:15.

*While Paul was waiting for them in Athens, he was great-
ly distressed to see that the city was full of idols. So he reasoned in the synagogue with the Jews and the God-fearing
Greeks, as well as in the marketplace day by day with those
who happened to be there* (Acts 17:16-17 NIV).

When the early church was faced with overwhelming opposition to the point of imprisonment and ultimately beat-
ings, they never raised their voice to attack the devil. Rather,
they prayed to God for strength to proclaim the Gospel with
boldness.

*"Now, Lord, consider their threats and enable your ser-
vants to speak your word with great boldness. Stretch out
your hand to heal and perform miraculous signs and wonders through the name of your holy servant Jesus." After
they prayed, the place where they were meeting was shak-
en. And they were all filled with the Holy Spirit and spoke
the word of God boldly* (Acts 4:29-31 NIV).

Demons in the air are not a threat to mankind. It is, in fact,
mankind who does not believe the truth, mankind who walks
in sin, mankind under the influence of demons who is a serious threat. Demons in the air are harmless. We *want* the
demons in the air, not in people, where they can inflict damage.

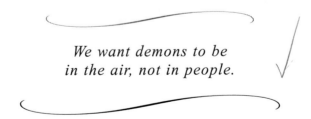

*We want demons to be
in the air, not in people.*

Demons are not a problem until they find people who will
yield to their destructive ideas and beliefs. The war that we

wage is not an attack against the devil as much as it is a message of truth to mankind. When man believes the truth, he will no longer give himself to the deceptions of the devil.

We must look at the New Testament and rethink our doctrines and methods of spiritual warfare and ask one question: "Is this based on the finished work of Jesus?" The answer becomes refreshingly obvious. Warfare today looks nothing like it did before the resurrection of Jesus.

CHAPTER 25

WINNING THE WAR IN YOUR SOUL

I f spiritual warfare does not take place in the "heavenlies,"
then where does it happen? If we do not fight the devil in
the air, where do we fight him? A person will always find the
wrong answer whenever he asks the wrong question. Satan is
already a defeated foe, so we do not fight him at all. We *resist*
him; we do not get dragged into a nonexistent battle. When
Christ sat down at the right hand of the Father, He signified
that salvation is complete. The battle has been won. Our Lord
and King led a triumphant procession over sin, death, and the
devil.

What we still have battles with are temptations, thoughts,
and desires. We all have felt oppression at some time or another. We know the voice of the enemy—or do we? There is a war,
yes, but the battle is not against the devil and the battleground
is not the "heavenlies." Our war is with our own beliefs,
thoughts, and emotions. The battleground is our mind. *"Dear-
ly beloved, I beseech you as strangers and pilgrims, abstain from
fleshly lusts, which war against the soul"* (1 Peter 2:11). We struggle in our minds and emotions when we are tempted or afraid.
The power that drags us into sin is not the devil; it is our own
desire.

For years Christians have violated one of the most common laws of emotional development. "To continue to do the

same things expecting different results is insanity."[1] We employ methods that still do not work. We refuse to stop using the same tactics. We even become offended when someone suggests that we should do something differently. We blindly continue on the same course expecting that this time it will produce the desired results.

One time while I was conducting a meeting, a young man jumped up and interrupted. He was passionately out of control at the mere suggestion that Satan was not our problem. When asked to be seated, he complied only momentarily before he was on his feet interrupting the meeting again. I have seen people become more passionate about this subject than almost any other. Yet, when you talk to some of these passionate people, you find that they have a very low degree of peace, success, and positive results from their efforts. Still, they keep trying.

I think that we all sometimes feel a little foolish over some of the extremes in which we have been involved. People have chartered planes and flown over cities to do war in the heavenlies. Others have gone on bizarre vigils for days. One man shared about going into his basement at night, putting on all of his hockey equipment, and doing warfare. I have even seen church services where everyone came dressed in combat fatigues. Although I have never gone to such extremes as these, I, like you, have done things that I would rather forget.

One night while praying for our city, this question came to mind: "If we have authority over the devil in Jesus' name, how many times do we have to bind him before it works?" Then I asked myself this: "If it does work, why does the devil

---

1. Source unknown. This is a common saying in all addiction recovery programs.

keep getting free?" These and many other questions caused me to reevaluate all the scriptures about warfare. The results were refreshing and produced victory.

Our Own Beliefs Can Hold Us Back

In examining all the New Testament passages concerning warfare, I found that when read in context, every one of them addresses the issues of self-control, thoughts, and emotions. In the years that have followed I have seen far more long-lasting results from teaching people to renew their minds than I have ever seen from long hours of "screaming at devils."

*Any truth that opposes the Word
of God is a vain imagination.*

When talking of demonic activity, I prefer to use the words *demonized* or *taken*. Our paradigm for possession prevents us from comprehending what is actually happening. When the Bible talks about being taken by the devil or demonized, it is usually referring to what is happening in your mind and thoughts. All the language literature about these words makes reference to the way the person is affected mentally and physically. In fact, one of the words for possession is the word *echo*, which means to hold back. A form of this word is used when speaking of someone having a possession, but holding back a part of it.

To be possessed (or taken) is a state where a person is affected in such a way that it results in being held back. It is important, however, to realize that the root of demonic activity is a matter of the mind, beliefs, and emotions. People who have limiting beliefs are demonized. They are held back by a belief that does not accept the promises of God. A hypochondriac is demonized; he is held back by the belief that he will find happiness or comfort from sickness. There are those who think it is the will of God to be financially lacking. People who think like that are demonized by their beliefs. Any truth that opposes the Word of God is a vain imagination, which renders a person demonized, held back, restricted.

> *And Jesus went about all Galilee, teaching in their synagogues, and preaching the gospel of the kingdom, and healing all manner of sickness and all manner of disease among the people. And his fame went throughout all Syria: and they brought unto him all sick people that were taken with divers diseases and torments, and those which were possessed with devils, and those which were lunatic, and those that had the palsy; and he healed them* (Matthew 4:23-24).

This passage refers to people being "taken" with sickness. People are often taken with sickness because they are first taken in their beliefs. For this reason we must follow Jesus' pattern to first teach the truth about the kingdom of God. Then He got them delivered.

There are people all over the United States who are *taken* with sickness. The problem lies more in their belief system than in their body. In our clinic we have found that a person who is chronically ill who does not respond well to treatment or keeps relapsing, must have a change of beliefs before he can improve.

We always find a faulty belief system in chronically ill patients. Some feel they are being punished by God. Others believe they are unworthy of health. Others are so ridden with guilt they cannot function. These people must hear the message of the kingdom of God in order to come out of their problems.

In 2 Corinthians 10:3-5 Paul said, *"For though we walk in the flesh, we do not war after the flesh: (for the weapons of our warfare are not carnal, but mighty through God to the pulling down of strong holds;) casting down imaginations, and every high thing that exalteth itself against the knowledge of God, and bringing into captivity every thought to the obedience of Christ."* Every limiting belief is a vain imagination. Every thought that does not promote and support the finished work of Jesus is a vain imagination. Vain imaginations are thoughts that exalt themselves above God and His Word.

The first real place of warfare will be in your belief system. The Bible tells us in Romans 12:2 to *"be not conformed to this world: but be ye transformed by the renewing of your mind."* For too long we have viewed renewing the mind as overcoming individual sinful thoughts. Although that is true—we do not need to be thinking those thoughts—they are only the fruit. Our belief system is the root. We experience growth and development as we accept the finished work of Jesus.

*A faulty paradigm is always
at the root of any individual problem.*

Your personal belief system determines your paradigm. Your paradigm controls how you interpret everything you see, hear, and experience. A faulty paradigm is always at the root of any individual problem. If I truly believe that God is for

— 133 —

me, I will be secure. If I truly believe that God loves me, I will have self-worth. When I am fully convinced that I am qualified for all the promises by the finished work of Jesus, I will be full of faith. If I deal with my global beliefs, the individual problems will be solved. Although we should no doubt deal with individual beliefs, the first place of warfare is our life-dominating views and opinions.

The Way to Win Every Battle

The first place of warfare should be you. *"Casting down imaginations, and every high thing that exalteth itself against the knowledge of God, and bringing into captivity every thought..."* (2 Corinthians 10:5). As new believers we should develop a new matrix of beliefs around which all our other beliefs revolve. It is a struggle to trust the wisdom of God and exchange our views for His. That is the *war in your soul.* It is challenging to dismiss those lifelong beliefs with which we have governed our life's decisions.

This scripture did not stop by saying to bring every thought into captivity. It says, *"...and bringing into captivity every thought to the obedience of Christ."* Too often we translate this verse to mean that we should stop every wrong thought. That's not what it says. We should capture it! If you have tried stopping it, you have found that it is virtually impossible to stop thinking about something by trying to stop.

In order to stop myself from thinking about my temptation, I have to think about it. It is a tormenting effort in futility. Try this experiment. Take an item, any item. Look at it. Think about it. Now set that item, whatever it is, out of sight. Tell yourself to stop thinking about it. You cannot stop. As long as you are trying to stop, you cannot stop.

We misunderstand the instruction in 2 Corinthians. We think the goal is to make our thoughts stop. It did not say to stop them. It said to bring them captive to *Christ's* obedience. "Can I make this thought obey me?" That is the wrong question. The question should be, "Did Jesus, in His obedience, deal with this issue?"

For example, let us say that you are facing a temptation. You ask yourself, "Did Jesus conquer this sin through His death, burial, and resurrection?" The answer is an overwhelming, "Yes!" Then, if Jesus conquered this, it has no power over me. In His obedience this issue was dealt with. This is bringing that thought captive to the obedience of Christ.

The Bible says that we experience salvation because we believe God raised Jesus from the dead and confess Him as Lord. Applying this principle quenches every question, every battle, and every temptation. "Did Jesus conquer this when He was raised from the dead? Is Jesus my Lord?" That settles every issue.

Paul said that when dealing with temptation one should...

> *Likewise reckon ye also yourselves to be dead indeed unto sin, but alive unto God through Jesus Christ our Lord. Let not sin therefore reign in your mortal body, that ye should obey it in the lusts thereof. Neither yield ye your members as instruments of unrighteousness unto sin: but yield yourselves unto God, as those that are alive from the dead, and your members as instruments of righteousness unto God. For sin shall not have dominion over you: for ye are not under the law, but under grace (Romans 6:11-14).*

The word *reckon* means to consider it so. Since we are dead to sin, we should simply consider it so. This is the way we resist sin. When we begin to scream at the devil and rebuke the sin, we are focusing on the sin. We are keeping it alive in our minds. Worst of all, we consider ourselves to be vulnerable and alive to this sin. We are not considering it as it is. If we reckon ourselves dead to sin and alive to God, it is a simple matter of yielding to righteousness that emerges from a heart full of faith.

A person may protest, "It is just not that easy. It cannot work this way." That person is in a war in the soul. He is at war with his beliefs and feelings about the finished work of Jesus. Fighting the devil will never resolve the issue of your personal beliefs. It will simply keep you so occupied with the devil that you never deal with the real issues.

At this point people often begin to scream at the devil and pray about the problem. All that does is simply magnify the problem. It ultimately promotes fear and a sense of desperation. The fact that you may shout out will momentarily affect your emotions and thoughts, but it will not change them. Shouting at the devil and experiencing momentary relief actually reinforces an already faulty belief system. It seems to work. You think that if you do it more, it will work longer.

Jesus has already won the battle with the devil. He stripped him and led him away captive. Satan is a defeated foe. He has no right to work in your life. Your battle is not with the devil. Your battle is with your beliefs. If you feel the need to shout at the devil, that is all right, but at some point you must renew your mind. You must put off those old thoughts and beliefs and renew your confidence in the finished work of Jesus.

If you bring the rest of your thoughts captive to what Jesus did, your life will take on a new dimension. If all your belief system is built on what Jesus has done for you, then you will discover what it means for Jesus to be at the center of your life.

When we trust the finished work of Jesus, we are infused with grace, peace, and joy. The battle is over; there is no more internal struggle!

CHAPTER 26

SELF-CONTROL: THE REAL WARFARE

The demoniac whom Jesus encountered on the shores of the Gaderenes prowled the tombs night and day and cut himself. He was what we would consider a madman. If there was any phrase to describe this man, it would be *out of control*. Our basic picture of a demoniac is of someone who has given his or her control over to another.

Self-control, on the other hand, is a fruit of the Spirit. It is an essential element for peace, victory, and success. Proverbs 25:28 says, *"Like a city whose walls are broken down is a man who lacks self-control"* (NIV). A city with no walls is defenseless against an attack. Likewise, the person without self-control is defenseless. He creates an opportunistic environment for the evil one.

Being Prepared to Stand

Ephesians 6:10-12 says, *"Finally, my brethren, be strong in the Lord, and in the power of his might. Put on the whole armour of God, that ye may be able to stand against the wiles of the devil. For we wrestle [struggle] not against flesh and blood, but against principalities, against powers, against the rulers of the darkness of this world, against spiritual wickedness in high places."* Transforming ourselves into soldiers dressed for battle is not the ultimate object of this passage. The more important lesson of this example is thorough preparation.

The purpose is not to go out to war. The purpose is to stand against the "*wiles*" of the devil. A wile is a deceit, a trap, or a "lying in wait." Satan is a deceiver. He has no power or authority. He relies completely on deceit. The way to stand against deceit is not to start a battle. That would actually be proof that we are deceived. To focus our attention on him is the ultimate deceit. No, the way to stand against deceit is to be completely established in truth.

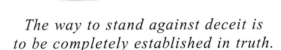

*The way to stand against deceit is
to be completely established in truth.*

Paul went on to say that we wrestle with principalities and powers. The wording of "*against principalities, against powers*" should really read "in regards to principalities and powers." It is not the same wording in the phrase, "*against flesh and blood.*" The words *principality* and *power* refer to position, rank, and right. We struggle with the idea that we can give Satan authority in our lives. But we now know that is not possible.

What did Jesus do with the position and authority of the devil and demons? He stripped them of all position, rank, and right. Then, when He rose from the dead in Matthew 28, He said, "*All power* [authority] *is given unto me.*" Our struggle is not against the devil as much as it is with our beliefs concerning his position, power, and authority.

Ephesians 6:13 continues, "*Wherefore take unto you the whole armour of God, that ye may be able to withstand in the evil day, and having done all, to stand.*" This actually says "and having *overcome* all." We will not stand if we overcome all; we will stand because in Christ we have overcome all. Because you have overcome all through the death, burial, and resurrection of Jesus...stand!

Verse 14 tells you how to stand. It says, "*Stand therefore, having your loins girt about with truth, and having on the breastplate of righteousness.*" Jesus is your righteousness. The breastplate guards your heart. Have your heart established in faith righteousness.

Verse 15 says, "*And your feet shod with the preparation of the gospel of peace.*" When Jesus came He took the entire curse of the law so that there would be peace between God and man. The foundation—the firm footing that is going to make you always able to stand—is a readiness of mind concerning the Gospel of peace. When trouble comes, if we do not maintain confidence in the fact that there is peace between God and us, we will not have the proper footing. We will fall.

Verse 16 says, "*Above all, taking the shield of faith, wherewith ye shall be able to quench all the fiery darts of the wicked.*" We do this "*above all*"! Faith simply believes what God has said to be true. If you do not have faith, you will not believe what God has done for you in Jesus. It matters little what God has done if we do not believe it.

"*And take the helmet of salvation, and the sword of the Spirit, which is the word of God*" (verse 17). Traditionally we viewed the sword of the Spirit as the weapon we would use to kill the devil. Throughout my years of study, I have found that Scripture is the best way to interpret Scripture. So when I look at the Scriptures to understand what this sword is, I find something quite different.

Hebrews 4:12 tells us about the sword of the Lord. It says, *"For the word of God is quick, and powerful, and sharper than any twoedged sword, piercing even to the dividing asunder of soul and spirit, and of the joints and marrow, and is a discerner of the thoughts and intents of the heart."* The sword of the Lord is what I use on my own thoughts and intentions to keep myself from being deceived.

Beating the Air Does No Good

In 1 Corinthians 9:24-26 Paul said, *"Know ye not that they which run in a race run all, but one receiveth the prize? So run, that ye may obtain. And every man that striveth for the mastery is temperate in all things. Now they do it to obtain a corruptible crown; but we an incorruptible. I therefore so run, not as uncertainly; so fight I, not as one that beateth the air."* This Scripture passage appropriately describes our current attempts at spiritual warfare. Beating the air is shadowboxing.

Our spiritual warfare
has been simply shadowboxing.

In shadowboxing you are swinging at an opponent who is not there. Your shadow looks real, but it is not. It cannot harm you. To shadowbox is a waste of time and energy. The activity may give you the sense of accomplishment, but it will not accomplish anything.

Instead of beating the air, Paul determined to put his efforts into that which would bear fruit. In verse 27 Paul said, *"But I keep under my body, and bring it into subjection: lest that by any means, when I have preached to others, I myself should be a castaway."* Paul was saying that he has to keep *himself* in line to have victory, not the devil. Paul was saying that he did not let his body get out of control.

The Bible says that you have a spirit of self-control. *"God did not give us a spirit of timidity, but a spirit of power, of love and of self-discipline"* (2 Timothy 1:7 NIV). The *King James Version* says *"sound mind,"* while *The Amplified Bible* says *"self-control."* A victorious life is one of self-control. This is how Paul kept from becoming a castaway. He did not do this through fighting with the devil. He used his faith to live a life of self-control and complete victory!

CHAPTER 27

THE DEVIL AND YOUR MIND

One area that we must address if we want to better grasp the realities of personal "warfare" is our thoughts. There are many different concepts concerning the source of tormenting thoughts. All too often our own beliefs about the origin of thoughts simply add to the torment.

Let us start our study in the book of Daniel, chapter 2. Daniel was in captivity in Babylon. King Nebuchadnezzar had a dream that troubled him, and he could not remember it. So he called for the sorcerers and magicians to tell him the dream and interpret it.

These were men skilled in the "dark arts." They were the elite in the world in their craft. With all their skill, however, they could not tell the king either his dream or the interpretation of the dream. In other words, Satan could not see into the mind of Nebuchadnezzar.

As we look throughout the Scriptures, we do not see a place where Satan can hear the thoughts of our minds. This tells me that Satan does not have the access to our minds as we once believed.

He could not interpret the king's dream in chapter 4 either, even after he knew it. So all this tells me that Satan does not know our thoughts and even when he does, he is not skilled at interpretation.

Satan, no doubt, can hear and see. What he can hear and see, though, are our words and actions. I do not believe he knows anything about what is in my heart until I verbalize or act on it. Therefore, I once again become personally responsible for my words and actions.

*Satan does not have the access
to our minds that we thought he had.*

Early in my walk with God I began to pray while facing a difficult situation. I called it praying, but it was really complaining to God. Just as I began to speak, I felt the Spirit of the Lord speak to my heart. He simply said, "Do not say what you are about to say. The information you give out will become the basis for the strategy formed against you."

After studying that concept in the Scriptures, I have never again had a fear of Satan being able to read my thoughts. That brings up the next question: "If he cannot read my thoughts, can he put thoughts in my mind?"

This is a legitimate question. It is probably a question for which we will never find a complete answer. We should, however, look to the Scriptures to find what we can. Otherwise, we enter the realm of conjecture and develop elaborate doctrines based solely on theory.

Can Satan Influence the Heart?

We have only one scriptural passage that makes reference to Satan's putting something in a person's heart. It is the case of Judas. The *King James Version* says that Satan *"put into the heart of Judas Iscariot, Simon's Son, to betray him"* (John 13:2). The *New International Version* says, *"The evening meal was being served, and the devil had already prompted Judas Iscariot, son of Simon, to betray Jesus."*

Now, we know that Judas was the treasurer. We also know that on occasion he would help himself to the money in the bag.[1] So, we know that Judas had a money problem. His greed created the opportunistic environment that made him vulnerable to the devil. The priests had previously made him an offer of thirty pieces of silver to betray Jesus. We know it was previous because he left the Last Supper to meet with them and betray the Lord. His greed made him vulnerable.

So how did Satan put this into his heart? Did he speak directly into Judas? Did he have knowledge of Judas' mind? In John 13:27 it states that Satan entered Judas. *"And after the sop Satan entered into him. Then said Jesus unto him, That thou doest, do quickly."*

We see several things in this passage. First we see that Satan does not have the capability to enter a person until that person first puts himself in a position where his heart is committed to the situation.

We can never know if Satan spoke directly into Judas' heart or if all the circumstances combined with the condition of his heart was the way he "put it in Judas' heart." But again, we know that Judas had to first put himself in this position through greed and murder before he was vulnerable to the devil. If Satan did verbally speak in his heart, it was the product of the heart reduced to actual demon possession. Therefore,

---

1.   John 12:6: *"This he said, not that he cared for the poor; but because he was a thief, and had the bag, and bare what was put therein."*

it is doubtful that Satan could speak directly into your heart unless you have given yourself over to him.

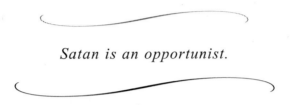

Satan is an opportunist.

In the case of Ananias and Sapphira, Peter said that Satan had *"filled"* their hearts. Once again we have to wonder, did Satan speak directly into their hearts or, as the original language indicates, were they simply under the influence of sinful thinking? We are left with the same unanswered questions and the same conclusions in that incident as well as in Judas'.

Like Judas, Ananias and Sapphira yielded to sin to such a degree that their own hearts killed them. We will never know whether or not Satan spoke directly into their hearts or if they simply yielded to an ungodly temptation. What we do know, unmistakably, is that they gave themselves over to sin and greed in a deliberate choice.

After examining these two passages we really do not know if Satan spoke directly into their hearts. While we should consider the possibility, we also should take a more biblically consistent view of the source of thoughts.

We Produce Our Thoughts

The Bible indicates the two sources of thoughts to be the heart and the mind. It is my opinion that our thoughts are "of the devil" any time they deny the Scriptures, oppose truth, or limit us in any way. However, the devil does not put these thoughts in our minds; we put them there because we believe the *"doctrines of devils"* (1 Timothy 4:1).

Our thoughts come from our memory and our imagination. With our memory we look to the past, and with our imagination we look to the future. Our imagination tends to spring out of our desires and beliefs. With our imagination we cultivate our future. We write new beliefs onto our hearts.

The imagination can conceive either faith or sin. The imagination is not evil unless we make it evil. If we use our imagination to give birth to our lust apart from God, we have used it for an evil purpose. We can, however, use our imagination to cultivate faith and confidence. With our imagination we can write new and empowering beliefs onto our hearts. We can see the unseen. We can remove the limits.

The greatest source of "voices in our minds" is actually memories. Memories are part of our destructive or empowering beliefs. Although volumes could be written about memories, I will try to limit this discussion to the roles memories play in our current thoughts.

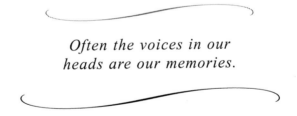

*Often the voices in our
heads are our memories.*

God taught man to use memories in a positive way. He often told the children of Israel to place a stack of rocks in a certain place. When their children asked the purpose of the monument, they were to remember what God had done for them and tell the stories to their children. In so doing they would not only teach their children, but they also would create associations.

God also told the Israelites to write Scripture on their walls, to wear it as frontlets before their eyes, and to fashion it into jewelry. Again, this would create memories and associations. Memories are important, but your associations created with those memories may be more important.

When we remember a particular event, we never just remember the event; we remember what experiences we have associated with that event. Every time we think of a certain situation, other neurological processes begin to bring forth data associated with that event. I can think of certain events from my childhood, and I can smell the aroma that was present at that time.

There are other events that I think of and begin to have physical sensations. When I am away from home and I think about my wife, I have physical experiences. I miss her and long to be with her. A dream is nothing more than a thought with a lot of associated experiences.

There are certain situations a person could encounter that would evoke associations with similar events. The moment this happens, the mind begins to run the neurological pathways that the memory relates to the event. For example, you might have had a bad experience with a past love. You meet someone new. This situation is really different. You have met the perfect person for you. This person loves and adores you. Yet, you have all these negative emotions when you are with this person.

The negative feelings and thoughts you are experiencing are associations. You associate love with your past negative experience. You think thoughts that are inconsistent with your current experience.

The super-spiritual interpretation of this would be to attribute the thoughts and emotions to an attack of the devil. The truth is that these thoughts and emotions are simply associations. Fighting the devil will not solve this problem. However, creating new associations will give you the desired results.

Thoughts and emotions go hand in hand. They function along the lines of a continuum. The Bible says each seed bears after its own kind, and that principle applies here as well. Whatever you think produces "like emotions." Likewise, whatever emotions you experience produce "like thoughts."

If you lived in a country at war, you would listen for the sirens to warn you of an enemy attack. Every time you heard the sirens you would run for shelter and hide. The sirens were the warning that the enemy was attacking. Then suppose you move to another country where there is no threat of war. All is at peace. Then one day you hear a siren. You would probably panic and run for shelter. All the emotions of the past would immediately come forth. But, in this country the siren is a call for the volunteer firefighters.

Associations can be very powerful. The thoughts we experience are often heard as words. These are, however, our thoughts. This is not the devil speaking into our mind. Any attempt to remedy this problem by entering into warfare with the devil would probably create new fears and anxieties.

Some assume that the relief they experience by rebuking the devil when having negative thoughts is proof that it is in fact the devil behind those thoughts. Actually, when we do anything drastically different, we interrupt the neurological patterns that our mind is starting to run. Therefore, our negative thoughts stop. We temporarily experience relief. But then the tormenting thoughts return.

Some have said, "I resisted the devil, and he just came back stronger." I cannot accept this as valid. The Bible says in James 4:7, *"Resist the devil, and he will flee from you."* It does not say that he will come against us stronger; it says that he will flee. Maybe what is coming back is not the devil. Maybe it is just those thoughts that you interrupted.

Finding the Cure

The Scriptures present a concept for dealing with problems that I call "put off-put on."

*But now ye also **put off** all these; anger, wrath, malice, blasphemy, filthy communication out of your mouth. Lie not one to another, seeing that ye have **put off** the old man with his deeds; and have **put on** the new man, which is renewed in knowledge after the image of him that created him* (Colossians 3:8-10).

The Scriptures say to stop stealing and start working. Stop lying and start speaking the truth in love. For every destructive act that we stop we must put on a life-giving action or belief. In the area of thoughts, interrupting the pattern is putting off the negative thought. Then the question is, "How will you replace that thought?"

If I fear for my safety, I must interrupt that thought pattern that is affecting my emotions and replace it with another pattern. This is where we put on scriptural-based beliefs. This is where I bring forth from the Word of God a verse or passage that promises me protection. This is a fix; this is not a cure. This will bring relief from the current situation but will not prevent its return.

To prevent the return of negative, fearful emotions I must write something new on my heart. The association of fear that I have with a particular situation was written on my heart with a combination of information and strong emotions. To change this belief I must meditate on the promises of God. I must see myself experiencing the promise, provision, or protection of God. I must see it so clearly that I create a new association.

I will only create a new association if I ponder the promise and can see myself experience it until I have strong, positive emotions. This is what the Bible calls meditation. When I have created this new association, it will be my automatic response when I am in a threatening situation. I will see myself overcoming and not losing. I will feel confident and victorious.

Believing the truth and writing it on your heart is the only way to stop the "voices" of doubt, fear, and destruction. The voices you hear are your own beliefs. They will change when you change your beliefs!

CHAPTER 28

WARFARE IN YOUR CITY

The next phase in warfare comes in taking your city. In the parable of the talents, Jesus said, *"Occupy till I come"* (Luke 19:13). The word *occupy* does not mean to merely hold on to what a person has. It means to be doing business and gaining ground. We are supposed to be using our talents (skills and resources) for doing business and gaining ground for the kingdom of God. We are supposed to gain and maintain ground in our family, our city, and our world.

Some portions of the church have translated "occupying" as something that is done inside the walls of the church. This is not the example set by Jesus or the church in the book of Acts. They prayed to God and evangelized the world. They did not scream at the devil. The New Testament pattern for warfare is to pray and go.

Proverbs 11:11 says, *"By the blessing of the upright the city is exalted: but it is overthrown by the mouth of the wicked."* To coin a phrase, Christians have become those who "curse the darkness, but seldom light a candle." It becomes easier to be the voice of doom than to become the beacon of light.

A blessing is speaking favorably over a situation. A curse is a spoken negative. A curse is when you speak death, destruction, negativism, fault-finding, and criticism. These spoken words have the potential power, when heard and believed, to bear fruit after their "kind." Jesus spoke a negative over the fig tree when He said, *"No man eat fruit of thee hereafter"* (Mark 11:14). The result was, the tree withered and died.

Our nation is withering and dying because of the lack of blessing and the abundance of cursing. Curses are self-fulfilling prophecies. We proclaim how bad it is, people hear and believe it, then they live it out.

We have a society built on doom and gloom. We watch news programs and feel the need to pray. After we pray, we continue to talk about how bad it is. We curse our city with the words of our mouths. It takes faith and love to stand in the midst of the darkness and show God's love to an undeserving world. If they saw it in us, maybe they would want what we have.

Our nation is in trouble because
we have cursed more than we have blessed.

Most of the world knows what the church is against. It knows the judgment that awaits the ungodly. But very little of the world knows anything about the love of God. Even if they hear us speak it, our actions deny it.

In recent years there have been times when I was ashamed to identify with certain Christian groups. I have watched on the news as groups did "warfare" against homosexuality and other sins. The end result was not people being saved and set free. The end results were reactions of anger and violence. All that the city's homosexual population knows, as a result of those types of meetings, is that the church is against them.

Real Warfare Is Preaching the Gospel

We need to stop screaming at the devil in the sky and spend more time proclaiming the Gospel of the Lord Jesus. We need to stop cursing and start blessing. The greatest example of this is in Acts 17. Acts 17:16 says, *"Now while Paul waited for them at Athens, his spirit was stirred in him, when he saw the city wholly given to idolatry. Therefore disputed he in the synagogue with the Jews, and with the devout persons, and in the market daily with them that met with him."* Paul did not attack the people. He did not wage a war to get the devil out of the sky. He did not even attack the people for their idolatries. Instead, he preached the Gospel.

He went into this city that was filled with idols. Instead of turning this into an opportunity to curse them, I like what he did in verse 23 of Acts 17. It says, *"For as I passed by, and beheld your devotions, I found an altar with this inscription, TO THE UN-KNOWN GOD. Whom therefore ye ignorantly worship, him declare I unto you."* He seized the opportunity. He did not curse them and tell them how wretched they were. He found a starting place and used it to proclaim the Gospel. He identified their needs and showed them the real way to meet those needs.

If there was ever a city that needed spiritual warfare, it was in Acts 4. The Sadducees heard about the people turning to Jesus. In a fit of religious jealousy they determined to stop the spread of the Gospel and arrested the leaders. Verses 6-7 say, *"And Annas the high priest, and Caiaphas, and John, and Alexander, and as many as were of the kindred of the high priest, were gathered together at Jerusalem. And when they had set them in the midst, they asked, By what power, or by what name, have ye done this?"* Peter turned this into an opportunity to proclaim the Gospel.

Instead of putting their attention on the devil, the early church put their attention on God. In verses 23-24 it says, *"And being let go, they went to their own company, and reported all that the chief priests and elders had said unto them. And when they heard that, they lifted up their voice to God with one accord, and said, Lord, thou art God, which hast made heaven, and earth, and the sea, and all that in them is."* When the people heard the threats, they turned to their source of strength. They did not attempt to fight with the devil.

They prayed, quoted Scripture, and in verses 29-30 said, *"And now, Lord, behold their threatenings: and grant unto thy servants, that with all boldness they may speak thy word, by stretching forth thine hand to heal; and that signs and wonders may be done by the name of thy holy child Jesus."* They did not retreat to the synagogue. They intended to go forth with more power. They did not want God to kill; they wanted Him to heal.

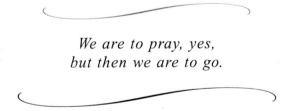

*We are to pray, yes,
but then we are to go.*

You may say, "That is what I have been praying." But, you are missing something. If you read on you will see that thousands of people were saved, which means that after they prayed they went out and proclaimed the Gospel.

The pattern of warfare for taking a city is to pray for boldness and pray for a plan. Then it implements that plan by going into the city. Get righteousness established in the hearts of the people. The righteous should become the politicians and leaders. The righteous should financially and personally assume the individual and corporate call of the church.

Even in the places where the Gospel is proclaimed, the ground is often lost because we fail to follow through with the rest of the plan. After people are won to God, they need to be discipled. They need to be equipped to become leaders of the city. The righteous should lead the way.

What Happens Depends on Who's in Charge

The book of Proverbs is the practical wisdom of God. You can take all the spiritual things you believe, run them through the book of Proverbs, and find practical application. Proverbs 10:16 says, *"The labour of the righteous tendeth to life: the fruit of the wicked to sin."* The Amplified Bible says, *"...the profit of the wicked leads to further sin."* Simply put, righteous people who prosper use their success to promote life and righteousness. When wicked people prosper, they use their wealth and influence to promote sin.

One of the greatest blasphemies in the world is the wealth of the wicked and the poverty of the righteous. The wealthiest, most influential people should be Christians. Because of vain imaginations concerning prosperity, we have given the wealth of the world to the wicked. The church failed to understand this simple principle. When the wicked have all the money, they would use that money to promote pornography, prostitution, alcohol, drugs, and every other evil.

When the wicked prosper in a city, there will always be more sin. They will use their prosperity to introduce perversion. The wicked seem to be more committed to their wickedness than we are to righteousness. The wicked use their influence to spread their values and beliefs. The righteous tend not to be as committed to spreading their beliefs and values.

One form of warfare is to give of your abundance to causes that are making a difference in the city and the world. We all should use our resources to do something meaningful for the kingdom of God. We should not bury our talent for fear of losing it. God provides seed for the sower. Those who choose to sow, prosper.

Proverbs 11:10 says, "*When it goeth well with the righteous, the city rejoiceth: and when the wicked perish, there is shouting.*" We will complain about the oppression of the wicked but seldom support the causes of the righteous. Righteous people should be in government and in business. We should influence the laws and policies that shape our city and nation.

Rather than using our beliefs as a basis of criticism against the lost, we should bless the lost by making safer cities. We should lead the way in social and environmental issues. We should be at the forefront of every just cause. We should be concerned about every issue that will benefit the quality of life for every person. This would be a warfare that would actually make a difference.

Christians seemingly have no have value for the lost. Why would a lost person want a Christian to be in a political office? We tend to have no value for a person unless he believes like we believe. That is why Christians are not in political offices. That is why Christians are not in positions of power. If, however, righteous people who love God and love people were in positions of power, it could go well in a city.

So how do we do warfare in the city? We prepare our hearts in prayer. We gain the ground by evangelism, and then we maintain that ground by raising up righteous leaders in every area of society.

CHAPTER 29

DEVIL MAGNETS

"Devil magnet" is not a term you will find in the Scriptures. It is my own tongue-in-cheek terminology for a person who lives in constant crisis and blames it on the devil. A devil magnet is a person who seemingly attracts "bad luck" and bad circumstances. If it can go wrong, it goes wrong for him. He is always living under some kind of attack. It is often people in these types of circumstances who perpetuate the myths about the power of the devil. It seems to be a way to explain their circumstance that sounds spiritual.

This person's problems are real. Their unwillingness, however, to look at their problems in light of the finished work of Jesus is the greater problem. It is the erroneous doctrine that emerges to justify our circumstance that often traps us in that circumstance. This "circumstance theology" is what I create to explain my circumstance. It is the unrealistic, unscriptural foundation from which many of my real problems emerge.

This circumstance theology doesn't come from people who want to be erroneous. They are saved, love God, and live a good life, but they need to justify their circumstance. I have ministered to some who believe they are under the curse. They believe the devil can attack at will. They never solve their problems, and they perpetuate spiritual myths about the devil.

The Bible says that God's people are destroyed because of a lack of knowledge.[1] Through this circumstance theology we create mystical concepts of God and the kingdom that blind us

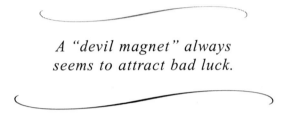

*A "devil magnet" always
seems to attract bad luck.*

to the knowledge that could set us free. In time, we have conflicting doctrinal positions. The simple truth is no longer understandable in the mystical maze of circumstance theology. Before long we have, as Paul put it in Colossians 2:19 (NIV), *"lost connection with the Head."*

The wisdom of God, on the contrary, is very practical. It is easy to understand if one simply believes. All understanding follows believing. If we do not believe the truth, we will never understand it in a way that is applicable to our situation. The New Covenant is not a mystery; it is a revelation. It clearly reveals God's perfect plan for man. It reveals how Jesus set us free from the curse of the law and the power of sin. It reveals how we can live the abundant life!

For What Are You Willing?

So the question remains, "Why do some people have so many things go wrong in their lives?" As simple as this may seem, it is often because they are willing for things to go wrong. Please note, I did not say they wanted things to go wrong; I just said they were willing for them to go wrong.

---

1.   See Hosea 4:6.

Many of the people who were or were not healed under Jesus' ministry had to deal with the issue of willingness. Although it is not abundantly clear in the *King James Version*, it is painfully obvious in the original language. God doesn't violate your will. If you won't choose it, God will not force it on you.

More than once Jesus looked at someone and said, "What are you willing that I should do for you?" Mark 10:51 is one example. *"And Jesus answered and said unto him, What wilt thou that I should do unto thee? The blind man said unto him, Lord, that I might receive my sight."* This is the same terminology used when people asked, "If You are willing, You can make me whole." Jesus asked this question because He could not heal a person who was not willing to be healed.

Why would anyone not be willing to be healed or to have an end to their life's problems? It is not usually the problem they want; it is something else. In Matthew 19:16-22 a man came to Jesus who wanted to enter the kingdom by his works. But when Jesus told him what he must be willing to do, he went away sad. He wanted his riches more than he wanted to be a child of God!

People who remain in destructive situations are getting something they want. The adulterer wants to experience something in his affairs, but he doesn't want to lose his family. When he commits adultery he is saying, "I am not willing for the chaos to end in my own family." No one wants financial pressure. We're all willing to give up the relentless barrage of bill collectors, but not if it means controlling our spending. No one wants the pain of their circumstances, but they want something else and the negative circumstances may simply be the fruit of something they are not willing to give up.

The Bible says, *"If ye be willing and obedient, ye shall eat the good of the land"* (Isaiah 1:19). Many declare they would obey if God would only speak to them. These very people sometimes pray day and night for a word from the Lord. But they already have a word from the Lord. When the Word of God states something to be true, God has already spoken. We, however, are not willing to take God at His word and apply His principles. The facade of waiting for God to speak is unbelief in what He has already spoken. We don't need for God to say again what He has already told us in His Word.

Accept Responsibility

There is a universal law of life that says that we attract things according to our attitudes. Jesus said this: *"For he that hath, to him shall be given: and he that hath not, from him shall be taken even that which he hath"* (Mark 4:25). In other words, whatever you have, you get more of. Whatever you do not have, you keep losing.

Devil magnets have a victim's mentality. They fear responsibility. They do not accept the difference between blame and responsibility. They would rather blame God, the church, or the devil than to accept responsibility. Responsibility does not belong to the person who will be blamed; responsibility belongs to the person who can solve the problem.

Job did not want to accept his responsibility in his problems. However, as long as he blamed his situation on God, he could not do one thing about it. The moment he stopped placing blame for what was wrong and accepted responsibility for what he could do, his situation changed. *"Wilt thou also disannul my judgment? wilt thou condemn me, that thou mayest be righteous?"* (Job 40:8)

You cannot solve a problem that you will not own. That is why 1 John 1:9 tells us, *"If we confess our sins, he is faithful and just to forgive us our sins, and to cleanse us from all unrighteousness."* To confess is to own. Confession is acknowledging that the sin is in fact ours. It is not about accepting blame; it is about accepting responsibility.

Responsibility belongs to the person who can solve the problem.

The person who attracts problems—the devil magnet—is the person who refuses to operate the principles of the kingdom of God and insists that he is being attacked by the devil. It is the person who is afraid to accept personal responsibility to believe and commit himself to the Word of God. His unbelief is a breeding ground for problems.

He may yell at the devil day after day, but he will not experience life until he submits himself to the principles of the kingdom of God. Life will be a weary, difficult process of warfare and battle trying to send away the demons.

Anyone can turn his circumstance around when he trusts the finished work of Jesus. Simply making decisions based on God's Word will end the majority of chaos in our lives. Jesus died so we could have abundant life. If you are not experiencing abundant life, go back to your source. He is able and willing for you to have all the promises of God. Are you?

CHAPTER 30

RESISTING THE DEVIL

One of the most encouraging scriptures concerning the devil comes from the writings of James. *"Submit yourselves therefore to God. Resist the devil, and he will flee from you"* (James 4:7). When we resist the devil, he has no option; he will flee. Some popular teachings present our conflict with the devil as a struggle wherein we invoke the name of Jesus repeatedly until we get the phrasing just right or until our faith reaches a high enough fervor, and then the devil finally leaves for a little while. This scripture did not say to rebuke the devil and he would flee. It said to resist him and he would flee.

Rebuking the devil seems to have its focus on attacking him. Resisting the devil, however, happens anytime we trust

Resist the devil by aligning yourself with the Word of God.

God. We can resist the devil without giving any thought or attention to him. Peter said it like this: *"Be sober, be vigilant; because your adversary the devil, as a roaring lion, walketh about, seeking whom he may devour: whom resist steadfast in the faith…"* (1 Peter 5:8-9). He said to resist him steadfast in the faith!

The word *resist* means to "set over against." We set ourselves against the devil when we align ourselves with the Word of God. Each time I make a decision or take a position based on trust in God and His Word, I am "set over against" the devil and his position. He flees because his lie has been exposed. He has no defense against the truth!

Faith Is, Regardless of the Outcome

The book of Ephesians says, *"Above all, taking the shield of faith, wherewith ye shall be able to quench all the fiery darts of the wicked"* (Ephesians 6:16). Faith in the Word of God quenches the fire in all Satan's darts. Lies are overcome as surely as water extinguishes fire and light overcomes darkness. When I trust God and His Word, I have destroyed Satan's every weapon and he has fled from my presence!

Faith is not as difficult as some may think. Faith is simply trust for God and His Word. Trusting God can often place us at the center of the real warfare—not the one where we fight the devil, but the one where I struggle with my opinions, desires, and selfishness. It is the struggle I have when my desires want to do it "my way"! Faith says, "I will follow God with my whole heart. I know I will emerge victorious no matter what comes my way."

Each time I make a decision based on God's Word, I put myself in direct opposition to the devil. I take myself to a realm where he has no influence or access. It is the kingdom of God! The kingdom of God is a realm that I can enter with each decision. Likewise, the world's system is a realm that I can enter just as easily. The principles and motives that guide my decisions place me in harmony with God or the devil. They place me in opposition to one or the other. There is no middle ground.

Jesus has called us to be believers and disciples. If we desire to participate in the abundant life, we must make our decisions based on His teachings and principles. It matters little if I pray and rebuke the devil. If I make selfish, unscriptural decisions, I align myself with him and the world's system. I usher in the fruit of his corrupt logic. Making decisions based on anything other than God's Word is tantamount to inviting the devil into my life.

Making decisions based on anything other than God's Word is tantamount to inviting the devil into your life.

Fortunately, we need not concern ourselves with the devil. We need not consider him in every situation. As a committed follower of Jesus, I must trust Him with my whole heart. I must bring every aspect of my life in line with His Word. I must build my life on His teachings and principles. Then I have no need to give the devil a second thought. I have raised the shield of faith and I have resisted him all in one motion. He always flees in defeat and fear when I trust God!

CHAPTER 31

THE POINT IS...

W e can get on with our lives. We can get on with God's call. We need have no fear or consideration of a defeated foe. We need not entertain any limitations based on our fear of the devil. God has given us everything that pertains to life. His resurrection has made all the promises ours. We have been made more than conquerors through Him. We are hid safely in Christ.[1] There should be no lack and no fear in our lives.

Isaiah 42:6-7, in the *New International Version*, says of God's call to Jesus, "*I, the LORD, have called you in righteousness; I will take hold of your hand. I will keep you and will make*

Jesus has opened our eyes.
We can see the devil as he is!

you to be a covenant for the people and a light for the Gentiles, to open eyes that are blind, to free captives from prison and to release from the dungeon those who sit in darkness." We have been liberated from all captivity. Jesus Himself ushered us into the light. Our eyes have been opened. The veil of the law has been removed so we can see God as He is. Jesus has conquered the

---

1.   See 2 Peter 1:3; 2 Corinthians 1:20; Romans 8:37; Colossians 3:3.

devil so we can see him as he is. He has given us the Holy Spirit so we can see ourselves as we are in Him. No circumstance can hold us!

It is impossible for us to move into our divine purpose if we are weighed down with the fear of the devil. We can be confident that Jesus fulfilled His mission. *"For this purpose the Son of God was manifested, that he might destroy the works of the devil"* (1 John 3:8). He sat at the right hand of the Father and said, "It is finished!" We can rest secure in His finished work!

The writer of Hebrews said it like this: *"Inasmuch then as the children have partaken of flesh and blood, He Himself likewise shared in the same, that through death He might destroy him who had the power of death, that is, the devil, and release those who through fear of death were all their lifetime subject to bondage"* (Hebrews 2:14-15 NKJV).

Because Jesus destroyed the one who had the power of death, we have no reason to live in fear. The very idea that we should continue to war against the devil exalts him above measure while undermining every aspect of our spiritual and emotional health. We have been set free in Jesus. We are free from death. We are free from sin. We are free from the devil. The Gospel of John says it best: *"If the Son therefore shall make you free, ye shall be free indeed"* (John 8:36).

Live a life of complete freedom. Fulfill your dreams! Trust God with all your heart. And rest safe and secure in the finished work of Jesus!

About the Author

Dr. James B. Richards is best described in one word: *pioneer*. Since 1972 he has proclaimed a message that is practical, relevant, simple, safe, and empowering. Through his personal, innovative, and sometimes outrageous ministry style, millions of people around the world have been drawn into a loving relationship with God while finding love and restoration in their personal relationships.

A best-selling author and successful teacher, theologian, and businessman, Dr. Richards is in high demand as a speaker and personal advisor to business people, clergy, and political leaders. His personal process of emerging from years of pain, dysfunction, and deep bitterness has given him proven tools for success in life, ministry, and business. Although he holds degrees in theology, human behavior, and medicine, his teaching is simple, well-rounded, understandable, and easy to apply. The results have been proven in nearly 30 years of personal, professional, and clinical application.